Russian Blue

Sphynx

Turkish Angora

Scottish Fold

Japanese Bobtail

American Shorthair

Singapura

Ragdoll

Snowshoe

Exotic Shorthair

Toyger

Chartreux

Norwegian Forest

Pixiebob

Oriental Shorthair

Siberian Forest

Cornish Rex

Abyssinian

Bombay

Siamese

American Curl

Devon Rex

Birman

Havana Brown

Chinchilla

Peterbald

Manx

Ocicat

Korat

Savannah

A WORLD OF CATS

For the cats, volunteers, and staff at
Good Mews Animal Foundation.

C.S.

To Morgan, Agatha, Dina,
Flora, Nina and Fergus.

L.U.

First published 2025 by Nosy Crow Ltd
Wheat Wharf, 27a Shad Thames,
London, SE1 2XZ, UK

Nosy Crow Eireann Ltd
44 Orchard Grove, Kenmare,
Co Kerry, V93 FY22, Ireland

www.nosycrow.com

ISBN 978 1 80513 613 2 (HB)

Nosy Crow and associated logos are trademarks and/or registered
trademarks of Nosy Crow Ltd

Text © Carlie Sorosiak 2025
Illustrations © Luisa Uribe 2025

The right of Carlie Sorosiak to be identified as the author and Luisa Uribe
to be identified as the illustrator of this work has been asserted.

All rights reserved.

This book is sold subject to the condition that it shall not,
by way of trade or otherwise, be lent, hired out or otherwise circulated in
any form of binding or cover other than that in which it is published.
No part of this publication may be reproduced, stored in a retrieval system,
or transmitted in any form or by any means
(electronic, mechanical, photocopying, recording or otherwise)
without the prior written permission of Nosy Crow Ltd.

The publisher and copyright holders prohibit the use of either text or illustrations to develop any
generative machine learning artificial intelligence (AI) models or related technologies.

A CIP catalogue record for this book is available from the British Library.

Printed in China following rigorous ethical sourcing standards.

1 3 5 7 9 8 6 4 2 (HB)

A WORLD OF CATS

A celebration of FASCINATING FACTS and
AMAZING REAL-LIFE STORIES for CAT LOVERS

Written by
CARLIE SOROSIAK

Illustrated by
LUISA URIBE

CONTENTS

A HEART FOR CATS	6–7
ARE CATS JUST LITTLE LIONS?	8–9
COME INSIDE, CAT!	10–11
WHY DO WE LOVE CATS SO MUCH?	12–13
SLEEPING, SQUEEZING AND CLEANING	14–15
TONGUES, TEETH AND TASTE BUDS	16–17
WHAT'S IN A WHISKER?	18–19
PAWS AND CLAWS	20–21
WHY DO CATS' EYES GLOW IN THE DARK?	22–23
HOW WELL CAN A CAT SMELL?	24–25
SLOW BLINKS AND CAUTIOUS SLINKS	26–27
THE MEOW AND THE PURR	28–29
WHAT DOES THE CAT SAY?	30–31
WHAT DO CATS THINK ABOUT US?	32–33
HOW CLEVER ARE CATS?	34–35
DO CATS HAVE FEELINGS?	36–37
WHAT DO CATS DO ALL DAY?	38–39
A NATURAL HUNTER	40–41
FERAL AND STRAY CATS	42–43
DIFFERENT KINDS OF CAT	44–45
WOW, LOOK AT THAT CAT!	46–47
THE FIRST BREEDS	48–49
HAVE YOU SPOTTED THIS CAT?	50–51

A WORLD OF CATS	52-53
CATS IN ANCIENT EGYPT	54-55
TALES OF ANCIENT HISTORY	56-57
ARE BLACK CATS UNLUCKY?	58-59
DO CATS HAVE NINE LIVES?	60-61
CATS RULE!	62-63
BRAVE CATS	64-65
CATS IN SCIENCE	66-67
CATS AND CULTURE	68-69
BIG-HEARTED CATS	70-71
THE RICH AND THE FAMOUS	72-73
DO CATS HAVE JOBS?	74-75
FEELING BETTER WITH CATS	76-77
FACT OR FICTION?	78-79
CATS EVERYWHERE	80-81
THE LAP OF LUXURY	82-83
CAT QUIRKS	84-85
CAREERS WITH CATS	86-87
WHAT TO DO IF YOU FIND A STRAY	88-89
A FOREVER HOME	90-91
EVERY CAT IS A GOOD CAT	92-93
GLOSSARY	94-95
INDEX	96

A HEART FOR CATS

What was your first word? Was it "mummy" or "daddy"? Was it "hi" or "bye" or "banana"? Mine was "kitty". From my earliest moments, I have always been obsessed with cats.

Growing up, my family had a gorgeous, long-haired grey cat called Bailey, who was very sweet-natured and didn't even chase mice. I learned to stroke her carefully, with awe, as she purred on the rug in our living room. I remember spending whole days just following her around the house, watching the tremendous swish of her bushy tail.

ALL IN THE FAMILY

Later came Bella, the smartest cat I've ever known. When my mum and I met Bella in her foster home, she'd managed to open the door of the upstairs bedroom by hanging on the handle with both front paws – I guess she was just excited to meet us! Besides her intelligence, what I first noticed about Bella was her toes. She had eight toes on each foot – instead of five – so her paws looked like tiny, furry mittens.

Immediately, I was fascinated by this. How many **polydactyl cats** – which I soon found out was the name for cats with extra toes – were there in the world? What was their history? And why had I never heard about them before? Soon, my research led to me learning about all kinds of cats, including ancient Egyptian cats, curly-haired cats and cats who star in movies.

Each one of these kitties is a little bit mysterious. Cats are good at being mysterious, from the way they skulk to the way their eyes glow in the dark. It makes sense that we have so many questions about them! Some of these questions are still unanswered, but every year, science teaches us new things about our purring, furry companions.

DISCOVERING A WORLD OF CATS

Now, I volunteer at a cat shelter, and I ask myself questions all the time. How are these shelter cats different from the big cats we see in the wild? Why does a cat's tongue feel like sandpaper? What does it mean when Patriot gives me a slow, careful blink? Sometimes, I'll sit on the shelter floor and just observe them – Santiago with her chatty meow, Cleocatra and her cautious slink, Mowgli and his love of feather toys – and think about what complex creatures they are. The more I learn about cats, the more amazed I am.

In this book, you'll discover some truly incredible cats: brave cats, wild cats and even a cat mayor! You'll meet **therapy cats**, impeccably groomed cats and cats with a taste for adventure. Each one of them will give you a glimpse into the fascinating life of our **feline** friends. You'll also find that human history – our science, our art, our culture – has kitty pawprints all over it!

ARE CATS JUST LITTLE LIONS?

Have you ever thought about where cats *come from*? Just as you have grandparents, and great grandparents, and great-great grandparents, cats do too! In fact, if we travel back 10.8 million years, we'll meet the very first ancestor – or relative – of today's cats.

ANCIENT CATS

Scientists aren't *exactly* sure what this cat-ancestor looked like – it's very hard to find kitty fossils that are millions of years old, as they're much tinier than dinosaur bones – but this creature was probably similar to today's panther. Imagine a large cat with a sleek body, pointy teeth and razor-sharp claws – a bit like the lions, tigers and leopards that you might see in the wild.

From there, it gets a little more complicated. There are 37 species in the **Felidae** (or cat) family, including everything from the broad, powerful puma to the teeny-tiny rusty spotted cat, which weighs in at around 1.5 kilograms when fully grown.

When we talk about species, we're talking about animals that have similar characteristics, and are similar enough that they can have babies with each other. It's one of the ways that scientists group animals together.

CAT-ANCESTOR   PUMA   RUSTY SPOTTED CAT

MIGHTY PREDATORS

New research shows that cats **evolved** from a much older creature. Here's the *Diegoaelurus vanvalkenburghae*, 42 million years ago.

WORLD TRAVELLERS

Each one of these 37 cat species is special and unique, and they come from all over the world. When the sea levels dropped roughly nine million years ago, allowing travel by land, cats packed their suitcases. Well, not *really*! But some did trot from Asia to North America, others to Africa, and over time the different species developed bodies and behaviours to fit in with their new environments.

The first ancestor of the domestic cat – also known as the house cat – came from the land surrounding the Mediterranean Sea, around 3.4 million years ago. This wildcat, called *Felis silvestris lybica*, was much smaller than some of its relatives, which served cats well many years later when they started to curl up in the laps of humans!

WILD AT HEART

So, is the cat on my sofa really just a little lion? Or a tiny tiger? Or a less-than-gigantic jaguar? There are some big differences, for example, lions can roar thanks to a special bone that holds up their tongues, and the cats on our sofas can't. But if you look *inside* all cats, their genes (the building blocks making up what they are) are very much alike. Genetically speaking, cats are 95.6 per cent similar to tigers.

SMALL CATS	BIG CATS	BOTH
Smaller	Larger	Have retractable claws
Have slitted pupils	Have round pupils	Groom themselves
Hunt alone	Hunt in groups	Play!

COME INSIDE, CAT!

So, how did cats go from roaming around in the wild to roaming around our living rooms? How did they make such a great leap – and when did this leap happen?

CAT FOLLOWS MOUSE

It all started with a mouse. Really, it did! Ten thousand years ago, in the **Fertile Crescent** – an area of the Middle East where the land was particularly good for growing crops – humans were busy farming. They were also building storerooms to bring their grain inside. Well, a certain rodent called the house mouse loved that! Inside, this little mouse could have a big feast.

But the house mouse wasn't the only creature looking for an easy meal. The domestic cat's wild ancestor, *Felis silvestris lybica*, was also prowling around the humans' villages. And he saw something interesting . . . tiny mice crawling into the grain stores! Like a good hunter, the cat followed.

Humans in the Fertile Crescent were very happy about that! These wildcats were skilled enough to catch mice, saving the grain, but they were small enough not to cause a lot of trouble. Plus, they were kind of cute!

TAMING OF THE CAT

The cats kept coming around, and the humans kept praising their efforts, perhaps giving them extra scraps of food in return. That was the start of cats' **domestication** – the process of turning a wild animal into a tame one.

Thousands of years later, it happened again in ancient Egypt. Around 3,600 years ago, that same type of wildcat began to help the ancient Egyptians with *their* pest problems. Scorpions, begone! Snakes, begone! These invaders were no match for the cat's claws and ancient Egyptians grew to appreciate their tiny kitty helpers.

Later, the ancient Roman army brought cats on their travels to scare pests away from food, and cats travelled on ships with the Vikings (who lived in Scandinavia from 800 CE to 1050 CE). Soon they were everywhere.

READY FOR BATTLE
Cats in ancient Rome didn't just protect the food stores, they also protected soldiers' armour! Ancient Roman armour was made of leather, and with cats around, rats probably thought before chewing on it . . .

OUTDOORS TO INDOORS

From the Fertile Crescent all the way up to the 1950s, cats largely lived outdoors. They roamed around in fields and patrolled villages. But nowadays, in many countries, our pet cats are just as likely to be found curled up in an armchair, softly purring by the fireplace or snoozing at the ends of our beds.

How did that happen? How did outdoor cats become indoor cats? It has a lot to do with litter trays! Until the 1950s, cats usually did their business behind a bush – or anywhere outdoors. Cat litter, invented by an American businessman in 1947, made keeping a cat indoors very easy – and much less messy! While many cats might prefer all the space and smells outdoors, others were very happy to trot into the living room: *Thank you, don't mind if I do.*

WHY DO WE LOVE CATS SO MUCH?

It's impossible to measure exactly, but some people estimate that there are around 700 *million* cats worldwide. That's a lot of whiskers flicking, a lot of tails flitting and a whole lot of purring. We see cats almost everywhere – and over time, they've come to form a unique bond with us.

On the island of Cyprus, around 9,500 years ago, a human and a cat were buried side by side, alongside a smattering of seashells. These twin graves – both facing the same direction – were a really important find, because they showed just how deep the human-cat connection runs. This human must've thought: *I love my friend so much, I want him with me forever.*

FUR BABIES

Why *is* our relationship with cats so strong? One of the reasons is that they're really, really cute – and they kind of look like human babies. Cats' eyes and faces are adorably round and their noses are as tiny as a button. Research shows that, when asked "What's cuter, a kitten or a baby?", most people think it's a draw! We want to nurture cats and kittens, just like parents do with their kids.

Have you heard the expression 'making biscuits'? This is when cats knead our tummies, their paws working away, which imitates how kittens get milk from their mothers. So, maybe they *do* think they're our babies! Even their cries – directed at humans – are at a similar **pitch** to the cries of human infants.

WHAT'S IN A MEOW?

Cats lack some facial features, such as inner eyebrow muscles, which both humans and dogs have, so it's tricky for us to read their facial expressions. But we can understand them in so many other ways – such as through their meows! Kittens meow at their mothers, asking for food, but adult cats – for the most part – meow only at humans. They are very cleverly trying to capture our attention, asking us to do something important: *Human, it's breakfast time. Fill my bowl, please!*

Cats have learned that a **soliciting purr** – a combination of a cry and a nice, humming purr – makes us act even faster, probably because it's less annoying than a normal meow.

And while we don't often meow back at them, we talk to our cats all the time! Cats *love* baby voices – high-pitched, non-threatening and sweet. They pay closer attention to the higher pitch, because it's outside of the normal range of speech. With baby talk, cats know we're speaking *specifically* to them.

YOU'RE BACK!

One recent study shows that most cats display **secure attachment** with their guardians, as most kids do with their parents or caregivers. This means, if a person leaves the room for a period of time and returns, the cat will notice them in a relaxed way: *I knew you'd come back!*

SLEEPING, SQUEEZING AND CLEANING

From the nearly hairless Sphynx cat to the stubby-legged Munchkin, our **feline** friends all look a bit different. Some tails are puffy, some are sleek. Some cats are longer and bigger, while others are more compact. But every domestic cat on the planet descended from the same wild ancestor, so they do have some things in common.

SPHYNX

MUNCHKIN

CATCHING SOME ZZZZS

Each cat begins as a kitten – a tiny, thinly-furred bundle, mewing for its mother's milk. Some kittens don't fully open their eyes for 16 days, but some start blinking at the world as early as 2 days old. Sleeping for up to 22 hours a day, they get the rest they need before starting to walk, play and bounce around at 3 to 4 weeks old.

Adult cats get plenty of beauty sleep too, snoozing for around 15 hours a day. They are most active at dawn (early morning) and dusk (just before nightfall), so lots of sleep helps them conserve energy for those times. Elderly kitties may need more sleep as they enter their twilight years.

NOODLE BODIES

Have you ever noticed how cats can fit into very tight places? That's because their bodies are really bendy, almost like noodles. They have very small **collarbones** – the curvy bones that connect shoulders to the rest of the body. In cats, these collarbones float freely, attached only by muscle. This allows cats to flatten themselves and *squeeze* through the tiniest window.

Cats' spines are incredibly flexible, too. Like us, every cat has **vertebrae** – back bones that make up their spine – but theirs are much more loosely linked than ours. So, they can twist and rotate, sliding under that chest of drawers with ease.

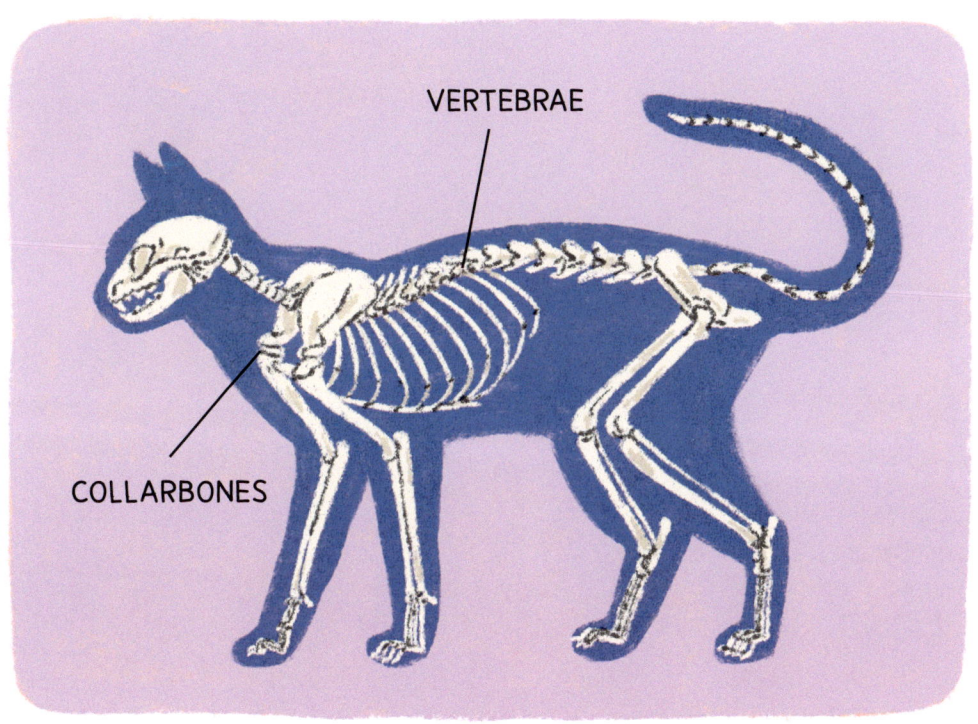

You might have heard that cats always land on their feet when they fall. And this is mostly true, thanks to their bendy bodies twisting mid-air to get themselves into the perfect position for landing.

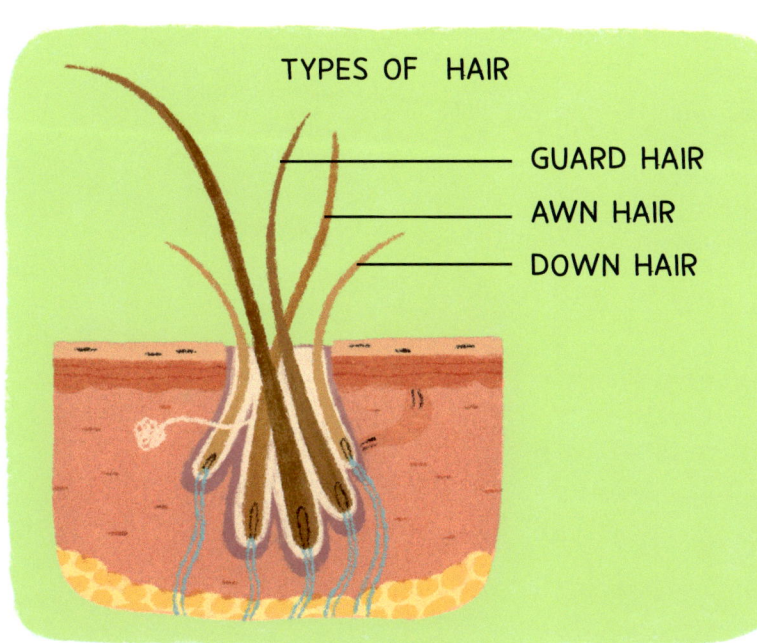

A NICE, CLEAN COAT

Is your cat long-haired? Short-haired? Medium-haired? However long their fur is, every strand is made of **keratin**, a protein that also makes up human fingernails. Many cats spend a quarter of their lives grooming themselves! After all, they do have millions of hairs to clean – and up to three layers of coat. Stiff guard hairs protect the cat, shorter awn hairs keep them warm and super-soft down hairs keep them *extra* warm.

Have you ever seen a cat licking her belly? She's grooming herself – removing dirt and getting rid of any dead hairs. Grooming, along with shedding, also helps adapt her coat to every season – less fur for the summer sun, more for the winter chill.

HAIRBALL!
Sometimes, cats swallow too much of their own fur and it forms a ball in their stomachs. This isn't good for their tummies so they vomit it up again. *Presto*, a **hairball**!

TONGUES, TEETH AND TASTE BUDS

Has a cat ever licked you? What did it feel like? Their tongue might have been rough and spiky, a little bit like sandpaper. There's a reason for that! Cats have prickly spines on their tongues.

SPINES LIKE A PORCUPINE

Imagine a porcupine's quills, sticking up everywhere. It's sort of the same on a cat's tongue, except the spines (called 'papillae') are teeny-tiny, and each spine curves *backwards*, the same as a hook. That way, with each lick, cats' tongues can perform amazing feats – such as scooping the tiniest fleas out of their own fur or grooming a **feline** friend.

Cats also use their tongues to lap up water when they drink, dipping them very quickly in and out of the liquid, and dragging a string of water into their mouths. Watch closely! Their tongues are lightning fast, darting up and down four times per *second*.

PAPILLAE

WHY CATS SKIP PUDDING

Do you have a sweet tooth? Maybe you love biscuits or cake or ice cream. Like us, cats have taste buds – little sensory organs that say: *Hey, I like this food*, or: *Yuck, this food is too bitter or sour*. They're all over the edges of their tongues.

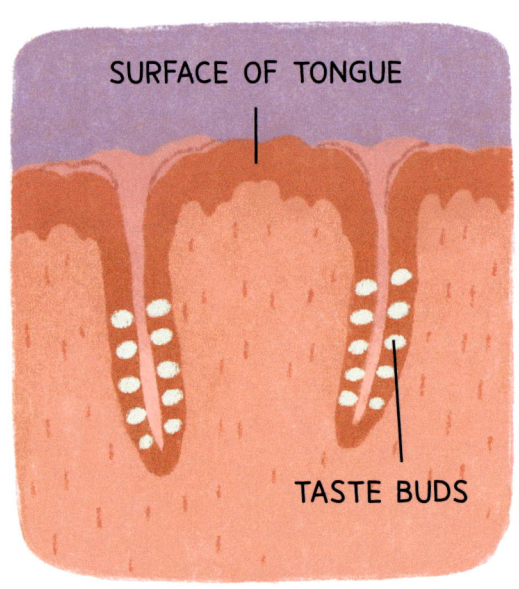
SURFACE OF TONGUE
TASTE BUDS

Unlike us, though, cats can't taste sweet things. Brownies? *Sorry, no*. Sorbet? *Nope!* Cats are **obligate carnivores** – meaning they need meat, not sweet treats, to survive.

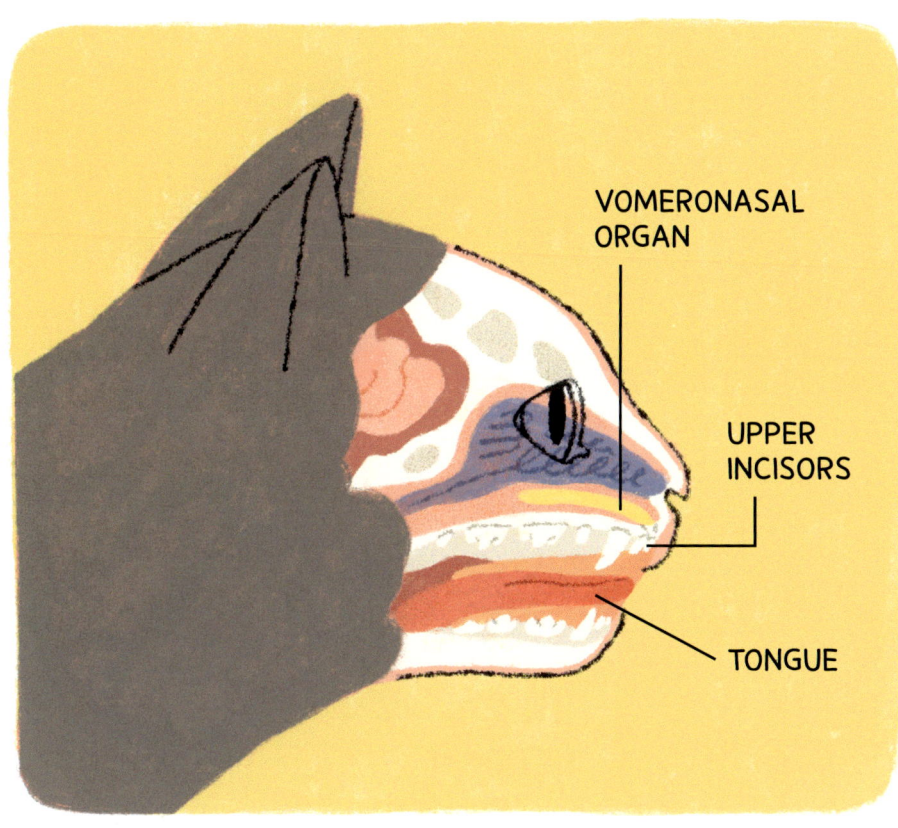

Felines *are* excellent taste-testers in other ways. Behind every cat's **upper incisors** (the teeth on the top row between the sharpest, longest teeth) are two small slits. When a cat opens their mouth and huffs in air, scent travels with it – going through the slits and into the **vomeronasal organ**, right above the roof of their mouth.

This special organ allows the cat to *taste* smells, extracting important information, such as: *That cat wee I'm smelling is from the **tortoiseshell** kitty who lives two houses away.*

HORSES DO IT, TOO!
This open-mouthed smell-tasting has a scientific name – it's called the **Flehmen response**, and cats aren't the only ones who do it! When a horse curls their lips and lifts their head, they're probably tasting the air. Same with camels, goats, elk and all sorts of other mammals.

PEARLY WHITES
Because cats are big meat-eaters, they need sharp, pointy **canine teeth** to tear meat apart, and **molars** and **premolars** to chew their food. Before they grow adult teeth, kittens start out with baby teeth, just like us. When their baby teeth fall out at around three to four months old, they sometimes swallow them! Interestingly, house cats never need fillings – their teeth don't have deep grooves, and cats don't eat sugar!

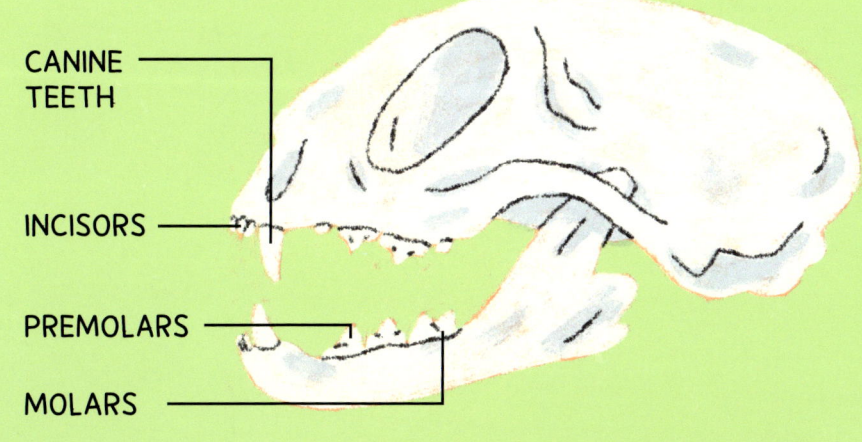

DON'T FORGET TO BRUSH!
Even if cats don't have a sweet tooth, it's still a good idea to brush their teeth. That will help with any dental problems later in life, such as decay from years of eating soft, wet food.

WHAT'S IN A WHISKER?

If you ask someone what's the coolest thing about a cat, they might say: "whiskers". The long, spindly plumes on a cat's face – and on other places, such as the back of a cat's legs – aren't just beautiful, they're also extremely important!

THE TIP OF THE ICEBERG
Made of **keratin**, whiskers are very stiff hairs that reach out into the cat's environment. Whiskers can tell: *There's a mouse rustling in that bush,* or: *Here is a piece of furniture that I'll manoeuvre around in the dark!* But how can whiskers tell these things?

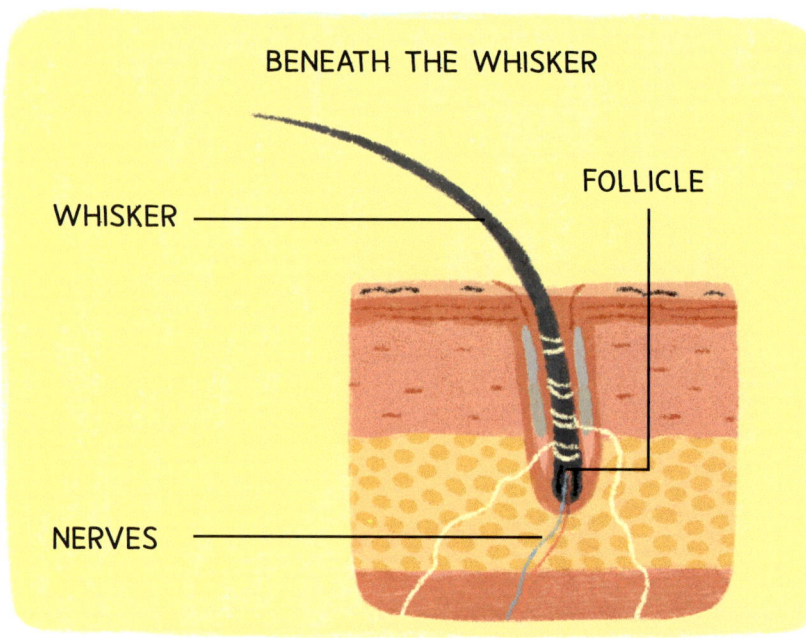

BENEATH THE WHISKER
WHISKER — FOLLICLE — NERVES

Each whisker grows from a **follicle** – a very sensitive organ in a cat's skin. These follicles are connected to **nerves** that send electrical signals to the cat's brain. So, if there's the tiniest change in air currents, for example, because a rabbit is twitching nearby, a whisker will vibrate, alerting the follicle. And *that* information will travel up to a cat's brain, which can piece together: *My whisker has vibrated because a rabbit is 30 centimetres away.*

NIGHT SENSES
Cats are **crepuscular**, meaning they're most active at twilight, when the light in the sky is fading. Whiskers help them *sense* their environments, especially when the sun isn't guiding the way.

BALANCE AND MOOD

Whiskers can also tell you a lot about how your cat is feeling. Relaxed whiskers are a good sign – your cat is calm and happy. If their whiskers are pulled back, watch out! You might have an annoyed kitty on your hands . . .

So, just as a cat speaks with their meow, they also speak with their whiskers – both to us humans and to fellow kitties.

HAPPY CAT

ANNOYED CAT

WHISKERS, WHISKERS, EVERYWHERE
Whiskers are all over a cat's body – on their chin, over their eyes, by their ears, on their forelegs. Look at a cat's chubby cheeks and you'll find 12 whiskers on each side and 3 sticking up from his eyebrows! Each plays their part in sensing a cat's world.

A MARK OF FRIENDSHIP

What if your cat rubs his face-whiskers and cheeks up against you? What's *that* communicating? Is he just itchy, and trying to get a nice face scratch? Could be! But cats also store **pheromones** (or chemical markers) in their cheeks and chins.

A rub from a cat transfers some of those chemicals over to you, onto your skin or your clothes. This is a kind thing! The cat is saying: *Hello, I'm greeting you, and you smell like me now – which means you're my friend.*

PAWS AND CLAWS

Are you right-handed or left-handed? Cats have a paw preference too! Males mostly bat at feather toys with their front left paws, while females mostly use their front right.

APPLAUSE FOR PAWS

Cats actually *tiptoe* everywhere. They walk on the very tips of their paws, stealthily, so they make less noise when they're sneaking up on **prey** – and so they can zip after mice, moles and shrews!

Watch a cat walking in the snow, and you'll discover something miraculous. Her back paws step in the exact same place as her front paws. This is called 'direct registering', and it doesn't just help a cat cover her trail, it's also really useful for balancing on narrow surfaces, such as the tops of fences.

Similar to whiskers, cats' pillowy paw pads pick up tiny vibrations in the environment. They can also detect temperature changes. If the street is too hot, a cat will think twice about strolling down it. When the weather is warm, their paw pads also excrete a little bit of sweat to keep their paws cool and lower their body temperature.

JAKE THE GREAT
While most cats have 5 toes on each front paw and 4 toes on each hind one, **polydactyl cats** can have more. A ginger **tabby cat** named Jake, who lived in Canada, had a record-breaking 28 toes, 7 on each paw.

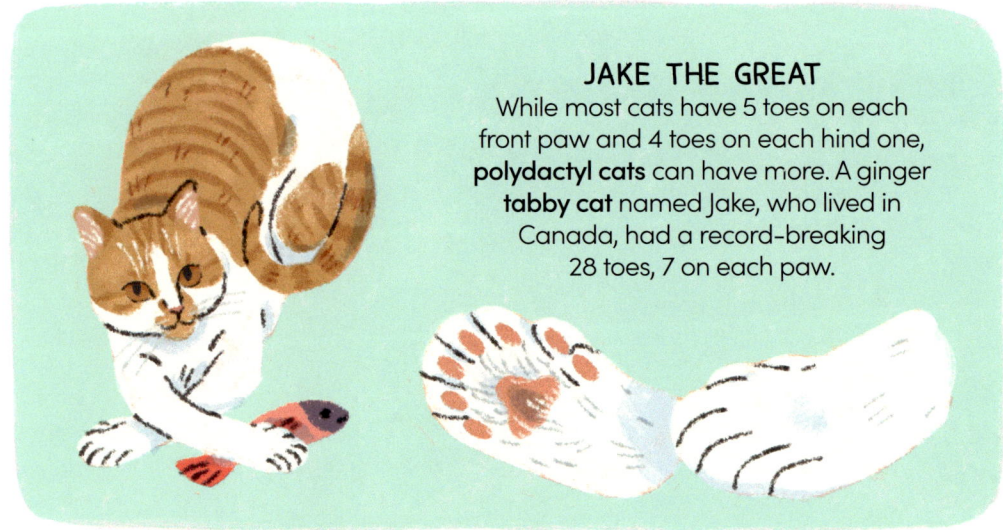

HELP, I'M STUCK!
You might have seen this on TV: someone calls the fire brigade because a cat is stuck up a tree! Cats are excellent climbers, thanks in part to their sharp claws, but claws only curve one direction – forwards. So, while cats can easily amble up a tree, getting down is much trickier!

HOW DO CATS KEEP THEIR NAILS SHARP?
You can trim a cat's claws with special clippers, or keep one or two **scratching posts** around, which will naturally file down their nails – keeping them nice and sharp. Otherwise, cats might use a tree or furniture to do this – such as comfy velvet sofas! They'll hook their claws into the material, pulling off the outer tip of their nails and revealing a super-sharp new layer beneath.

A cat's claws aren't the same as a human's fingernails – they're more like knuckles, growing from their bones. Cats use their muscles to control the movement of their claws, retracting them in and out whenever needed.

And cats need them *a lot*! Not just for climbing, but for holding onto food, hunting and telling other cats, *back off!* That's why declawing a cat – removing a cat's claw structure, including the nail bed, claw and bone – can be particularly harmful. The cat feels like they can no longer defend themselves – and it makes them walk differently, more painfully. People might declaw a cat so that they don't scratch humans or furniture, but declawing is not the same as trimming a cat's nails – at all!

WHY DO CATS' EYES GLOW IN THE DARK?

If you have a cat, pick a moment when they're feeling relaxed and look closely into their eyes. How are they different from ours? Well, for starters, they might be yellow or orange, and instead of a circular pupil at the very centre, cats have slitted pupils, like crocodiles and goats.

NIGHT VISION GOGGLES

Slitted pupils allow light into a cat's eye – and they get *really* wide if it's dark outside. That way, as much light gets in as possible. Cats can't see in pitch-black darkness, but they can see amazingly well in low lighting. Over the centuries, their eyes have **evolved** to hunt in the dimmest hours of the day – picking up *six times* as much light as humans see in twilight.

When it's sunny, those slits become thinner, blocking out the brightness. Their vertically shaped pupils also help with things such as **peripheral vision** and focusing on small **prey**, such as mice.

A CAT'S EYES IN THE DAY

A CAT'S EYES AT NIGHT

GLOWING EYES

Another reason why cats can see so well in the dark is their 'tapetum lucidum', a reflective layer at the back of their eyes that acts like a tiny mirror. Have you ever taken a picture of a cat and noticed that their eyes are glowing? That's the flash from your camera bouncing off the eye mirror! The tapetum lucidum helps the cat's eyes absorb even *more* light from the bounce-back.

High-visibility jackets and markers on our roads do the same thing, in a less complicated way – taking in light and shining it back at us.

BRIGHT IDEAS
In 1933, a man in Yorkshire in England was having trouble driving through a storm – it was terribly foggy – and then, he saw the eyes of a cat, staring out at him through the mist. *That's it!* he thought. Thus, **cat's eye reflectors** were born – road markers that guide traffic in low light.

BABY BLUES

Every single kitten is born with blue eyes, but as they grow up, their eyes might change to yellow or orange or even green. The true colour will be obvious by the time they are eight weeks old. It all depends on how much melanin (or pigment) they have in their irises (the coloured parts of the eyes). If a cat's eyes stay blue throughout their life, chances are that the cat's fur is white. White cats have less melanin in their eyes *and* coats.

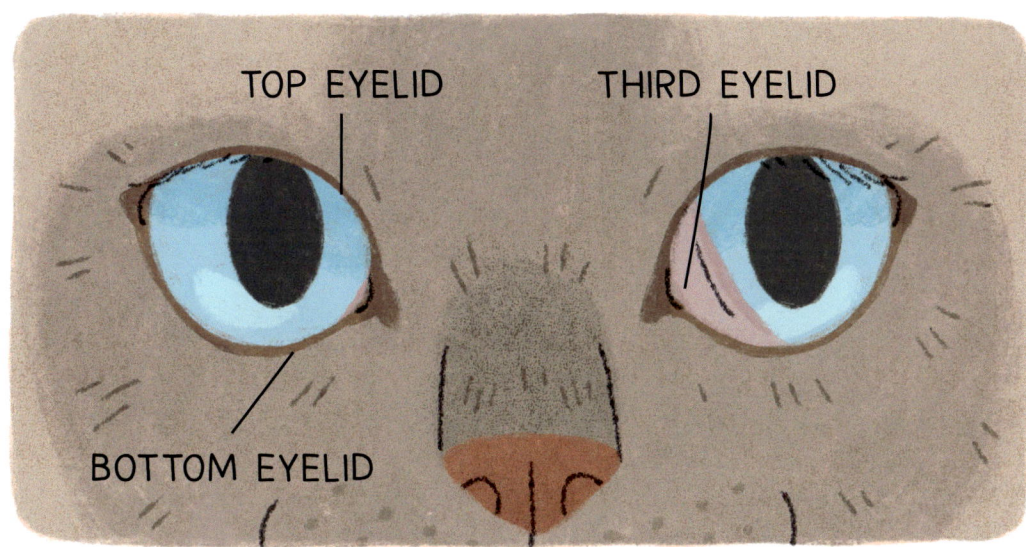

Speaking of colour, cats *can* see it! For years, scientists thought that cats might only be able to see shades of grey, but it turns out they can probably pick up on blues, greens and yellows. Unlike humans, cats have *three* eyelids – the upper, the lower and a third filmy one that swipes across their eyes. This acts like a windshield wiper, swiping away particles of dust and dirt.

LISTEN TO THIS!

Kittens are not only born blind, they're also born deaf. Both their eyelids and their ear canals are shut, to protect them from dirt, bright things and loud things. They can't even hear their mother's purr! So, it's amazing that, later in life, their hearing is so sharp, especially for quiet and **high-pitched** sounds, such as – you guessed it! – the squeaks of mice.

Thirty-two miniature muscles in cats' outer ears allow for an 180-degree swivel, meaning they can pick up on every sound in the kitchen: *Mmm, the plink of cat biscuits! Breakfast!*

HOW WELL CAN A CAT SMELL?

Newborn kittens might be blind and deaf, but they can find their way around thanks to their fantastic sense of smell. Even the tiniest kittens can tell where their mother is, just by her scent.

THE POWER OF SMELL

A cat can smell around 14 times better than you can, because accessing a wide variety of scents is an important **feline** skill. After all, you probably aren't stopping at every bush, sniffing for a trace of Alfredo, the local tomcat – but your cat certainly might be! That scent isn't just a smell – it's a message. It's chock full of information, such as: *This is my* **territory**.

To pick up on this information, cats use 200 million **olfactory receptors** – special parts of their body, found in the nose, that translate odour particles into scents. Remember, cats are also 'tasting' scents using an organ on the roofs of their mouths, so it's almost like they have two noses!

When they stick their faces into their bowls at dinner time, all of the good smells are hitting their nostrils. They're probably thinking: *Mmm, salmon! Mmm, chicken!* A cat's sense of taste isn't nearly as strong – so smell helps make up for it.

CATNIP OR ORANGES?

So, what scents do cats like best? Many go wild for **catnip** – a type of green plant containing a chemical that stimulates a cat's brain and makes them happy. A little more strangely, some cats are comforted by the scent of their own wee!

NO BITES
Researchers have just discovered that, if a cat rolls in catnip, she's much less likely to be bitten by mosquitoes. It's like a natural repellant!

On the flip side, many cats hate certain scents. Thyme or lavender? *No way!* Oranges and clementines? *Forget about it!* Citrus is a big *no* for kitties.

NOSE PRINTS

Have you ever heard that no two snowflakes are the same? That's also true for cats' noses. The outside has a particular pattern that's unique to that cat.

Look at the colour of a cat's fur – this might tell you what colour her nose is. It will usually be the same! Black cats almost always have black noses, for example. If the cat's fur has many colours, the nose might follow a similar colour scheme!

Sometimes, though, a cat's nose can change colour – just for a little while. Thanks to a surge in blood flow, a cat's pink nose might turn red if they're excited.

SLOW BLINKS AND CAUTIOUS SLINKS

From eyes to tail, there are so many different things that cats say with their bodies.

TAILS TELL TALES
You might think a wagging tail is a good thing, but that low, flicking tail could mean: *I'm in pain*, or *I'm really focused on something that I'm about to attack*, or *Please go away*.

LEAVE ME ALONE

I'M HAPPY TO SEE YOU

If a cat strolls up to you with her tail held high, then she's probably feeling confident – and is glad to see you! She might rub her face on your shins, purring. Interestingly, lions also keep their tails high and proud in friendly greetings.

If a cat is a little nervous because she doesn't know you – sometimes, it's hard to meet a stranger! – then her tail might be a bit more horizontal. Or, she could have a question mark for a tail – curved like a 'c' at the end. Cats' tails can literally ask the question: *Am I safe here?*

I'M UNSURE

BALANCING ACT
Besides the Manx, which is naturally tailless or stubby-tailed, all cats use their tails for balance. Puffy or spindly, the tail makes up 10 per cent of a kitty's skeleton system.

26

PUFFING UP

Always look out for a cat's fur. Is it slicked down on their back, laying flat on their tail? Then it might be okay to approach them. But if a cat's spine is arched, and his fur is puffing up with it – all along the back and tail – then it's best to give that kitty some space. Some cats get startled very easily, and their tails puff up so much they look like feather dusters.

THE CROUCH AND THE ROLL

If a cat is really scared, she'll probably freeze – crouching or puffing up on the spot. However, cats who feel uncomfortable might also scarper, slinking close to the ground. That way, their bellies and all their most important organs are protected, and they can get out of there *fast*.

Whether or not a cat shows you her belly can be a really important sign. Imagine you're playing with a cat, dangling a mouse toy above her face. If she rolls on her back, exposing her tummy, that usually means she trusts you!

THE SLOW BLINK OF LOVE

Have you ever noticed a cat blinking very slowly at you, with her eyes squinted? For years, cat owners have said this is an expression of love from their cats – and now science has proved that yes, kitties are showing affection or friendly feelings with these slow blinks.

The best thing is, research shows that if you do the same thing – slowly blink back at a cat, with your eyes sort of sleepy-looking and half-closed – they'll pick up the message! It's as if you are saying: *I appreciate you, too.* This works for house cats, street cats and any other cat you meet!

THE MEOW AND THE PURR

When asked "What sound does a cat make?" most people will naturally say, "Meow!"

BIG TALKERS
Is your cat meowing by the back door? Maybe she wants you to let her into the garden. Is she meowing by the cupboard with the fishy treats? That's also a clear sign! Basically, if the meow is directed at us, it could be a simple *hello!* or, it could be a command for something, such as food or attention.

Is a cat more likely to meow at another cat, or at a human? *Definitely* at a human. **Feral cats** – who haven't had much, or any, contact with people – meow far less than house cats, who are used to hanging out with us.

Just like each nose print is unique to each cat, there's a lot of variety in the meow. Some cats' meows are quieter and shorter, others are louder and longer. Some are lower **pitched**, some are higher pitched – and some cats are much chattier than others!

A CAT'S VOICE
No matter the sound, all meows come from the same place – the **voice box** (also known as the 'larynx'), located at the top of the throat. When air passes through the voice box, folds of tissue (called 'vocal cords') vibrate. This vibration produces sound – a cat's meow and purr.

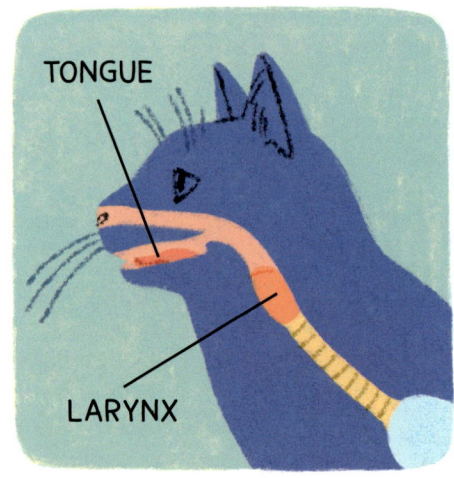

NO PURRING FOR YOU!
Did you know that big cats, such as lions and tigers, can't purr? This is because of a special bone in their throat that makes purring impossible – but helps them to roar.

WHY DO CATS PURR?

Have you ever had a cat curl up on your lap, and suddenly there's a tiny motor going? She's happily purring away, her entire body vibrating. One of the main reasons why cats purr is happiness. Social contact, such as stroking, cuddling and food-offering, is super important for cats because it helps them feel safe, comfortable and connected to people.

Cats purr when they're feeding their kittens – possibly to be *louder* than them, so that **predators** can't hear the tiny, nursing kittens. They also purr when they *are* kittens, telling their mothers: *I'm over here!* Adult cats sometimes purr if they're sick, injured or stressed, such as when they're in the waiting room at the vet.

CAN CATS HELP ASTRONAUTS?

Scientists have wondered for a long time why cats purr when they're not feeling their best. One theory is that a cat's purr can actually help their bodies to heal. When a cat purrs – inhaling or exhaling air through their voice box – it produces sounds waves that are powerful enough to help strengthen their joints and bones. Because cats spend so much of their time sleeping, purring might be a way of keeping their muscles and bones active, without using a lot of energy.

Some scientists are trying to figure out how to use this 'purr power' for astronauts, whose bones can become weaker on space flights.

WHAT DOES THE CAT SAY?

It's not just the meow and the purr. Cats have a whole language of their own – and it's really complex! For example, dogs have around 10 different sounds – including barks and whines – while cats have *at least* 27. From their friendly gurgle (which almost sounds like a human gargling water) to their soft trill (which cats use as a greeting), a cat's vocabulary can tell us a lot about what they're thinking. Sometimes, cats will string together a variety of sounds, such as a surprised hiss, followed by a throaty growl, followed by a teeth-baring snarl. That's like a phrase, or even a whole sentence!

WHEN FUR FLIES

Sounds such as hissing and growling usually come into play when cats don't get along with each other. This often happens when **territories** are involved. Cats mark their spaces with their scents but neighbourhood cats might test the boundaries, wandering in. The home-territory cat might hiss at the intruder, expelling a long burst of air from his mouth. Sometimes, cats fight each other with their claws and their teeth, howling.

Cats howl for other reasons, too. They might be wandering around the house at night when suddenly, the lights go out and everything is quiet. The humans have gone to bed, but the cat doesn't know that: *Where'd everybody go? Am I all alone?* Let the wailing begin!

Many cat sounds begin in their throats, but sounds like the hiss and the harsher, shorter spit are 'voiceless', meaning cats use only air to make the sound, not their voices.

SAY IT – AND SPRAY IT
Occasionally, cats decide to *really* mark their territory. The tail will stick up straight in the air, quivering, and the cat will release a wide spray of wee, like a sprinkler. Impressive!

MURMURS AND SQUEAKS
Even if some cats fight, others get along swimmingly! And they have the language to show each other interest and affection. A young cat will approach another cat, murmuring, to ask: *Hey, you want to play?* Female cats will gurgle at their kittens, which might be translated as: *There you are! I like you.* And two kittens might face each other, squeaking, before pouncing on each other in play.

MAY I LICK YOUR HEAD?
Cats show their love for each other with their voices – and also with their tongues. If you've ever seen two cats cuddled up together, one licking the other's head, then you know those kitties are connected in a special way. Grooming each other is a way to show that they care about each other.

WHAT DO CATS THINK ABOUT US?

Humans are a big part of cats' lives! Cats snuggle in our laps, head-butt us and weave through our legs when we're trying to make a tuna sandwich in the kitchen. But how much do they understand about us?

A LITTLE MISUNDERSTANDING

The first thing you need to know is that cats probably think humans are cats. They don't look at us and go: *Oh, that's a person.* They think: *That is a much taller, possibly sillier, friendly cat.*

The fact we're not walking around on four legs with fur covering our bodies makes no difference. To them, we provide food – like mother cats – and we hang around in a friendly way – like kitty siblings. So to them, human equals cat.

One theory for this misunderstanding is the way cats have been **domesticated**. Dogs were trained to do specific jobs for humans, such as pulling sledges or helping blind people, but cats weren't bred for anything other than catching mice. They never exactly figured out – like dogs did – that humans are a totally different species.

AN IMPORTANT GAZE

Still, cats have managed to form special bonds with us – for example, when we point at food, their gaze follows. This is actually pretty incredible! Not even chimpanzees, who are very intelligent, can do this. Cats can understand our body language – that we're directing them towards something that might help them. They might think: *Mmmm, a tasty snack on the counter. Thanks, tall cat!* Even more amazingly, if you just look at the snack, a cat will still understand that your *eyes* are signalling a direction.

TRUSTING EYES

Cats can talk with their eyes, too. When a domestic cat encounters something a bit new and frightening – such as an open umbrella in the hallway – they might look back at their human for reassurance, asking: *Do you know what this is? Is it safe?*

That's called trust. A cat who trusts you *definitely* knows who you are – even if he thinks you're a cat. All cats can distinguish their humans from a stranger walking down the street.

HUMAN EMOTIONS
A recent study showed that our cats can pick up on our emotions – such as the sadness on our faces and the anger in our voices – and react to them. They might think: *Oh, you seem a bit down to me. I'm going to keep you company* or, *You're smiling! I'll come a little closer.*

WHAT'S IN A NAME?

While cats are more likely to respond positively to familiar humans than strangers, a cat still knows her name. Even if a stranger calls out "Here, Sooty! Dinner!", her head might lift at the sound as she thinks: *That's me!*

HOW CLEVER ARE CATS?

Nora, a grey **tabby cat** from the United States of America, rose to fame on the internet when she was taught to 'play' the piano. It made a lot of people wonder, just how intelligent are cats and what else could they do?

UNWILLING SUBJECTS

It's a hard question to answer, because cats don't like taking part in research experiments. Whenever scientists try to tell them what to do – "Hey, over here! Try this puzzle!" – cats usually leap in the other direction. Cats aren't the most patient of animals – and human activities can bore them.

However, we do know something about their brains! Cats have very developed 'cerebral cortexes'. That's the part of the brain that deals with things such as problem-solving and memory.

STEPPING INTO A MEMORY

One study – where the cats did cooperate! – shows just how interesting cat memory is. It turns out, for a cat to remember an object, such as a child's toy left in the middle of the room, they have to *interact* with it – not just see it. If a cat steps over a toy with her forelegs, she'll remember that object for a long time.

And she'll remember you, too! It's a common belief that cats can recall people for years and years.

SEEING GHOSTS?
Have you ever seen a cat following something *really* closely with her eyes, but when you look in the same direction, there's nothing there? Some people believe that cats can see ghosts! Scientifically speaking, cats have great visual intelligence. They might be looking at a teeny-tiny bug, or a speck of light, that our eyes – and our brains – don't notice.

CAT TRICKS
A lot of the time, cats won't ask for help. When researchers give dogs a hard puzzle, dogs will look back at the humans like they're saying: *Assist me with this task!* Cats won't. If they feel like taking part, they will attempt to solve the puzzle independently.

Of course, cats will work with humans – when they want to. And you can train them to do fun tricks! The Amazing Acro-Cats, an acrobatic troupe of rescue cats based in Chicago in the United States of America, proves this beautifully. While the cats sometimes wander off into the audience, or decide, *Nah, I'm not doing that trick tonight*, they can also jump through hoops, push tiny shopping trolleys and balance on balls.

Any cat has the ability to learn. Some cats give high fives, others play fetch and some have learned to use toilets instead of the litter tray!

DO CATS HAVE FEELINGS?

For a long time, people thought that cats – as tiny, wild **predators** – didn't feel many emotions. But that's completely false! Just like humans, cats experience a wide range of feelings, from sadness and anxiety to joy.

BEST FRIENDS

Sometimes, two cats will form such a close bond with each other that they become what is known as a **bonded pair**. When this happens, animal shelters will make sure that the two cats are adopted together. Placing them in different households would make them miss each other too much and each cat might get depressed after the separation.

DEALING WITH LOSS

When someone who's close to a cat dies – another cat, a person, or even a dog in their family – the cat may hide, or mope around the house, or start to act oddly. She might start batting cutlery off the table or peeing outside of her litter tray. That's grief. That's a cat saying: *Things are different now, and I don't like it.* Like humans, cats will usually learn to adjust to the loss after some time has passed.

WHAT'S CHANGED?

Cats like their routines – and anything that disrupts that routine can make them very nervous. Maybe there's a new baby in the family, or builders are hammering away next door.

And what do cats do to calm down? Sometimes they lick themselves, but they might lick themselves *too* much. They also might stop eating for a little while, or spend their days hiding under the sofa. Some nervous cats might need extra space, while some might need extra cuddles! To help them, keep their routines normal where you can.

THE LOVE EFFECT

Now comes the biggest question of all – can cats feel love? Do they adore us like we adore them? Well, it's really hard to measure love – but science shows that cats form very deep attachments to humans and each other.

When a human baby is born, a hormone (or chemical message) called **oxytocin** is released in the brains of both the baby and the parent. This hormone bonds them together, so when they look at each other, they feel love! The same thing can happen between cats and people. Stroke your **feline** friend, and oxytocin is released in both your brains.

GOOD FUN
A kitty slinks up to another cat, swats that cat's tail and runs away. That kitty is saying: *Chase me, chase me!* Cats like to play fight and roll around together, just as much as they enjoy batting at feather toys. They might not laugh like we do, but they certainly know how to experience fun!

WHAT DO CATS DO ALL DAY?

A cat meows at the back door, tail high, begging to go outside. When the door opens, the cat slips into the garden, leaps over the fence, and goes . . . where? What does a domestic cat do with her time?

INDOOR CATS

For inside-only cats, the answer is a little easier to discover. We can see them racing down the hall, chasing a toy mouse or curled up in a ball on the sofa, snoozing away. But what cats do when they're out of our sight has long fascinated scientists and cat owners alike.

KITTY MYSTERIES
Before GPS collars, cats' daily routes were a mystery. There are still a lot of mysteries surrounding cats! Such as, why do only some cats react to **catnip**? Who knows!

CAT TRACKERS

Over the years, there have been several studies on the movements and habits of outdoor cats. Researchers use GPS collars – which fit snugly but safely around the cats' necks – to track their routes with computer technology.

These studies show that some cats wander up to 3 kilometres away from their houses – that's the length of 125 tennis courts! – and patrol specific routes daily or weekly. On these routes, they mark things with their scents – the corners of houses, fences, hedges – sending the message: This **territory** is mine! Other cats, stay away!

OUT ON THE TOWN
In a study from Germany, one cat often returned to the abandoned warehouse where he was born. Another cat liked to follow his owner into town, joining them at a local café, while another hung out with the two other cats in his household – snoozing in the sunlight near each other.

STAYING LOCAL
Sometimes, cats might go over to the neighbour's house for a tasty treat. Other times, they just hang out in their own gardens, soaking up the sun. Older cats might not stray too far from home, while younger cats – who are more nimble – might test their limits and go a little further.

WHY DID THE CAT CROSS THE ROAD?
In places such as London in England, busy roads can be a hazard for outdoor cats. Some cats are smarter and like to look both ways before crossing the road – which is good! – while others will bolt out and hope for the best. Cats can't really sense how fast a car is travelling, but their sensitive paw pads *can* pick up if a car is nearby, or if traffic is heavy.

A NATURAL HUNTER

Before cats had nice humans providing them with meals, they had to hunt for food. While big cats such as lions often hunt in groups, the domestic cat manages alone.

SPRINGING AND SPRINTING

Even sleepy, sofa-loving cats have all the built-in skills of a natural hunter. Just look at their claws, which can pierce skin and hold food, and their ears, which can swivel in the direction of mouse-like squeaks. Their bodies can slink down low in long grass, barely noticeable, their sensitive paw pads hardly making a sound.

Part of the reason cats are such good hunters is their flexibility. They can follow mice into the tiniest of spaces. But their extra-bendy spines also give them speed – stretching, stretching, *stretching* while the cat is running – so that cats can get the most length out of every stride. Usain Bolt, one of the fastest men on Earth, once ran at a speed of 44.7 kilometres per hour. A domestic cat can run at a speed of up to 48 kilometres per hour.

Not only that, cats can jump up to six times their height. If the same applied to you, that would mean you could jump from the ground onto the roof of a two-storey building!

SOMETHING TO CHATTER ABOUT

Imagine a cat and a bird perched on either side of a window. The cat's tail is twitching, his pupils are wide and his jaw is opening and closing rapidly in a quick *chatter, chatter, chatter*. He's making an interesting sound, teeth clicking together, as if he's imagining the taste of the bird. Perhaps he is! That chattering might signal: *I'm frustrated that I can't reach that bird!* or *I'm excited, that little bird is so close to my teeth.*

ON THE HUNT

Cats *enjoy* hunting. They get to use all of their skills and senses for tracking and chasing, which is thrilling for them. That's why lots of cats hunt even when they're already being fed by humans. They have been known to capture everything from lizards to squirrels and from mice to birds. Sometimes, they'll bring their **prey** back to our homes, dropping them on our doorsteps as if to say: *Look! I've returned with something special.* These 'gifts' might be for us – or maybe cats feel safer snacking at home.

TOP SPOT FOR TOWSER

Towser, a **tortoiseshell** kitty who was born in Scotland in 1963, holds the world record for the most mice ever caught – a whopping 28,899 over the course of her life.

MORE MEAT!

Of course, this isn't so good for the animals that cats hunt. Every year in the United States of America, house cats prey on up to four *billion* birds, and in the United Kingdom, one study suggested that they are catching around 250,000 bats a year – which is a real problem! They're certainly not eating all of those birds and bats, mostly just catching them and lowering local wildlife populations.

Some people think that all outdoor cats should be kept in at night, when they are most likely to hunt. Another solution, according to one study, is to feed cats extra-meaty meals! You can also play with them more, with toys that *act* like prey. May I suggest a laser pen?

41

FERAL AND STRAY CATS

Many cats have human guardians – people who feed them, give them a home and sometimes clean up their poo! But some cats live on the street, or in the countryside, without a person or a family to care for them.

WHAT'S THE DIFFERENCE?

Stray cats once had contact with humans but are now out on their own. Sadly, some cats are abandoned by their humans, or have a human who becomes too sick or old to look after them.

Feral cats are cats who've experienced far, far less contact with humans. They've probably seen some humans – but maybe they've never been stroked, cuddled or fed directly by them.

There's a tiny window in a cat's life – from around 2 to 14 weeks old – when they learn to get along with humans. If a cat doesn't meet any humans in that time then it'll be harder for them to trust people as they get older. Feral cats might hiss if a human tries to approach them, saying: Who are you? What do you want from me?

SCRAPS AND NIBBLES

How feral and stray cats live depends on the country. In countries such as Montenegro, with a huge stray cat population, some shop owners leave out small dishes of food and water. In India, groups of cats often hang out near food stalls, nibbling on the scraps. Some of these cats might be semi-feral – they haven't ever had a proper home, but they've had a *little* bit of interaction with humans – and they might even take a treat from the palm of your hand.

If food is scarce, some feral cats resort to eating from the rubbish, which isn't great for their health.

HELPING HOMELESS CATS
Many charities throughout the world are set up to help these stray and feral kitties. The charities provide things such as **vaccines**, as well as special operations that stop cats having babies – kittens that would need homes, too.

CAT COLONIES

Stray and feral cats may live alone, but you might also see groups of cats living together – say, in a local park or behind a supermarket. This is called a **cat colony**, and the group could include up to 15 cats – mostly females and their babies. Colonies tend to group around food sources, such as that nice-smelling fish and chip shop down the street, where there are lots of titbits.

THE CASTLE KITTIES

Disneyland, in California in the United States of America, is home to the famous Mickey Mouse. And you should know by now that wherever mice go, cats follow! Around 200 feral cats are currently prowling around Disneyland, living in the nature outside the rides and exhibits.

Some call them guardians of Disneyland's castle, because they 'protect' the area from mice. Not Mickey – but actual pests that invade the property. Disney even has a plaque for these kitties, celebrating their valuable service!

DIFFERENT KINDS OF CAT

The Russian Blue is such a striking cat – with short, silvery fur and intense, green eyes. You definitely wouldn't confuse it with a Sphynx cat! Those kitties are naturally hairless, with skin that wrinkles like a raisin. Even though every cat has similar traits, from their flexible spines to their sensitive whiskers, there are some big differences between breeds.

PEDIGREE OR MOGGY?

So, what are we talking about when we say 'breeds'? Well, a breed is a specific type of cat that looks – and usually acts – a certain way. For example, the Scottish Fold has little folded-over ears and often has a bit of a stubborn streak, while the Ragdoll – who is incredibly fluffy, with eyes as blue as the ocean – will go limp (like a ragdoll) in your arms when you pick her up. Going limp doesn't mean they're ill, they're just very relaxed!

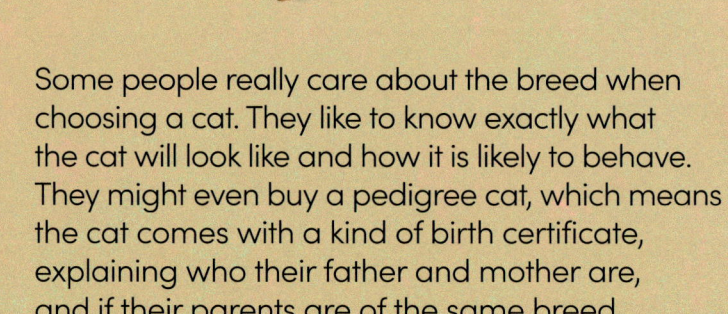

Some people really care about the breed when choosing a cat. They like to know exactly what the cat will look like and how it is likely to behave. They might even buy a pedigree cat, which means the cat comes with a kind of birth certificate, explaining who their father and mother are, and if their parents are of the same breed.

But there are lots of cats who are a mix of breeds – sometimes, *many* different breeds. In the United Kingdom, these '**mixed-breed**' cats are often called **moggies**. Around the world, they have different names – in Mexico, they're called 'gatos mestizos' and in Japan, they're called 'roji no neko' (alley cats). These kitties can make fantastic companions.

TABBIES, TORTOISESHELLS AND MARMALADE KITTIES

According to the International Cat Association, 73 different breeds of cat exist – from the flat-faced Persian to the large-eyed Australian Mist – but we often talk about cats by mentioning their coat patterns or colours, not just their breeds.

For example, **tabby cats**! They are not a breed, but all tabbies have tiny 'M' markings on their foreheads, and their coats can be a swirl of colours and shapes, from black patches to brown stripes.

WHERE DO PEOPLE GET THEIR CATS?
Cats arrive in our homes in all sorts of ways. Often, they're adopted from shelters, or from family and friends. Sometimes they are even rescued from the street. It feels good to give a kitty a safe home.

Ever seen a pair of tortoiseshell glasses? They are a mix of two colours – such as orange and brown – with white. You can find the same pattern on a **tortoiseshell** cat. Almost all of them are female. And almost all marmalade (or ginger) kitties are male!

A WALK ON THE WILD SIDE
A hippopotamus can't have a baby with a giraffe. However, house cats and wild cats share so many genetic features (how their bodies are made up) that some of them can have babies with each other. These babies are called 'wild hybrids.' One of these hybrids is the Savannah cat, which is part domestic cat, part serval (a wild cat native to Africa).

Is breeding wild hybrids responsible? There's a big debate about that! Lots of people don't understand how challenging it is to care for them, and many believe that wild animals should stay wild.

WOW, LOOK AT THAT CAT!

Huge cats, hugely old cats, hugely furry cats – the kitty world is full of extremes.

CORNISH REX TO MAINE COON

All kittens are tiny when they're born, but some **breeds** naturally stay small, even as they age. A regular-sized cat will tower over a Singapura, a Cornish Rex or a Munchkin – three of the littlest breeds. Lilieput, a **tortoiseshell** Munchkin from California in the United States of America, is one of the smallest cats on record – due to her short legs, she only measured 13.3 centimetres from paw to shoulder!

MUNCHKIN — 12 to 18 cm
SINGAPURA — 15 to 20 cm
CORNISH REX — 20 to 30 cm
NORWEGIAN FOREST CAT — 23 to 30 cm
TURKISH VAN — 25 to 35 cm
MAINE COON — 40 cm

AVERAGE HEIGHT FROM PAW TO SHOULDER

Then we have the kitties that can stop people in their tracks at cat shows. Norwegian Forest cats, Turkish Vans and Maine Coons spring to mind. The average Maine Coon stands taller than the average Dachshund, and most Turkish Vans weigh twice as much as Chihuahuas.

THE LONGEST

One of the world's longest ever cats was a Maine Coon with a long name. He was known as Mymains Stewart Gilligan – or Stewie for short – and hailed from Nevada in the United States of America. Stewie's guardian knew her cat was special. When she held him up to show off his magnificent length – from the tip of his head to his tail – people stared at him with awe. Measuring an astounding 123 centimetres long (about the height of a seven-year-old child) Stewie liked to strut around the local elderly care home, where he worked as a **therapy cat**, putting a smile on the residents' faces.

CAT DOGS
Maine Coon cats are named after the state of Maine in the United States of America, where they were originally found. They're like the Golden Retrievers of the cat world – super sociable and friendly, and just as gentle as they are giant.

THE FURRIEST
The honour of longest fur goes to Sophie, a black, white and beige beauty from California in the United States of America, whose tail fur grew to be an extraordinary 25.7 centimetres long! That's longer than two fizzy drink cans, stacked one on top of the other.

THE OLDEST
How long a cat lives depends on a lot of factors, but many kitties live into their late teens, or even their early twenties. Two cats have topped the official chart – 38-year-old Creme Puff and 34-year-old Grandpa Rex Allen. Interestingly, they were both cared for by the same person!

What's their secret to long life? Their guardian, Jake Perry from Texas in the United States of America, said it's all about diet. These kitties didn't just eat cat food. They got home-cooked meals, including turkey bacon, eggs and even coffee with cream – don't try this with your kitty at home! At night, they relaxed in a special home cinema, watching nature documentaries – keeping their brains engaged.

THE FIRST BREEDS

Some **breeds** of cat – such as the American Curl, bred in the 1980s for its curled-back ears – are relatively new. But other breeds have been pouncing, meowing and coughing up **hairballs** for thousands of years. Who were these first cats?

CAT MUMMIES

As the second civilization to **domesticate** cats, the ancient Egyptians – who lived in northeast Africa from 3150 BCE to 30 BCE – are extremely important in kitty history. Sometimes, after they died, ancient Egyptian cats were mummified – their bodies wrapped in linen and prepared for the afterlife – along with their human companions. Look at artwork from this time period, and you might spot . . . spots! A little silver cat marked with black spots and stripes often appears.

These spotted cats look very similar to today's Egyptian Mau – a fitting name, since 'Mau' is an ancient Egyptian word for 'cat.' Tourists often see them wandering around Giza, Egypt, near the Great Pyramid. Could these kitties be directly related to the cats in ancient Egyptian artwork? Maybe! That would make them the oldest breed of cats in existence.

A CAT . . . FAIRY?

Another ancient cat who is still around today is the Norwegian Forest cat. The immense fluffiness of this cat's coat, perfect for winters in freezing cold Scandinavia – where temperatures can drop to -50 degrees Celsius! – gives it an almost magical presence.

Throughout history, many people have believed this cat really *did* have astonishing abilities. The Vikings, who lived in Scandinavia from 800 CE to 1050 CE, thought these cats might actually be *fairies*. How else could they be such excellent rock climbers? According to Norse mythology, the Norwegian Forest cats were friends of Freya, the goddess of love and marriage.

PAWPRINTS ON POETRY

Occasionally, literature gives us a hint about which cat breeds existed in the past. There's a Thai book of poetry – dated between the 1300s and 1700s – that's called *Tamra Maew*. Translation? *The Cat Book of Poems*. Inside, what looks like a Siamese cat prowls along the page.

These cats are called 'Siamese' because they originally hail from Thailand – which changed its name from 'Siam.' But these kitties have a long history in the United Kingdom, too. The kittens of Pho and Mia – the first Siamese cats brought to England – were put on display in 1885 at a cat show held at the Crystal Palace in London. Onlookers could get a close-up view of their striking blue eyes, dark-brown tails and magnificent ears.

LOST TO HISTORY

A few breeds, such as the Chinese Lop-Eared cat, are curious cases. Did this cat with the long, floppy ears actually exist? Between 1656 and 1938, several people claimed to have spotted one. A museum in Germany even placed a stuffed example of the breed on display. But this might have been a fake, or another type of cat or another type of animal altogether. Mythical or not, the Chinese Lop-Eared cat is definitely no longer with us today.

HAVE YOU SPOTTED THIS CAT?

Around the world, you can find **tabby cats** on many street corners. There might be a Siamese or a ginger **moggy** living next door. But some kitties are much rarer – more difficult to spot.

THE BLUE CATS OF FRANCE

Let's travel back to 1558. A French poet called Joachim du Bellay is observing a blue-grey, chubby-cheeked cat. The poet's pen scratches across the paper, describing the kitty's sleek fur and the way he so skilfully catches mice. This, probably, is the first written mention of the Chartreux – a beautiful cat with broad shoulders and orange eyes. Look at him quickly, and he almost seems to be smiling.

Some say that the Chartreux lived with monks in the 1700s, explaining why these kitties are so silent – sometimes monks are, too! Others say that it's more likely that these cats travelled from Syria with people who came to fight in wars between 1095 and 1291. Chartreux is also a type of woollen fabric from Spain. That special blue fur . . . it looks kind of woolly, doesn't it? Maybe that's where the name of their **breed** came from!

During the Second World War, there was less food around and it was harder for people to keep their pets, so spotting a Chartreux became rare. Until . . . wait a second! A whole **colony** of them was discovered, living outside a remote island hospital. They are still around today, but have stayed a rare breed ever since.

CURLY-HAIRED CATS

Other rare cats are newer to the world. The LaPerm wasn't 'discovered' until 1982. In Oregon in the United States of America, two cherry farmers were walking along their land. "Look!" shouted one of the farmers. "Speedy gave birth to her kittens!" Speedy was their barn cat. Over the following weeks, the six kittens' fur started to grow, but one kitten looked a little different to her brothers and sisters. Her fur was curly! Thus, the first known LaPerm was born. This won't surprise you, but the farmers named her . . . Curly.

A STYLISH HAIRDO
On humans, a perm is a special chemical process that makes straight hair form waves or curls. That's why the name 'LaPerm' makes sense for a curly-haired cat! The Cornish Rex breed, from Cornwall in England, has similar fuzzy spirals.

HAIRLESS CATS

Just over ten years later, the Peterbald burst onto the scene. While the curly hair on the LaPerm happened naturally, the Peterbald's baldness was created by humans. Cat breeders (people who pair up cats to have kittens) said, "Hey, let's cross an Oriental Shorthair and a hairless Donskoy and see what happens!"

Named after the city of Saint Petersburg in Russia, where this cat was first bred, most Peterbalds are hairless . . . which means they get chilly quite easily! This isn't ideal for freezing cold Russian winters. There aren't many Peterbalds around the world – they're pretty pricey! – but if you see one, offer her a heated cat bed, and maybe a jumper.

A WORLD OF CATS

Except for Antarctica, at the very tip of the Southern Hemisphere, you can find house cats in every corner of the globe.

FROM BRAZIL TO ETHIOPIA

Depending on where you live in the world, cats are treated a bit differently. Some countries have traditionally viewed cats as bringing bad luck, while in others, such as Ethiopia, they're not as popular as other animals, such as chickens or goats. But homes around the world are still bursting with cats. In Brazil, you can find a cat in 18 per cent of households – from apartments in cities such as São Paulo to houses in tinier, more traditional villages.

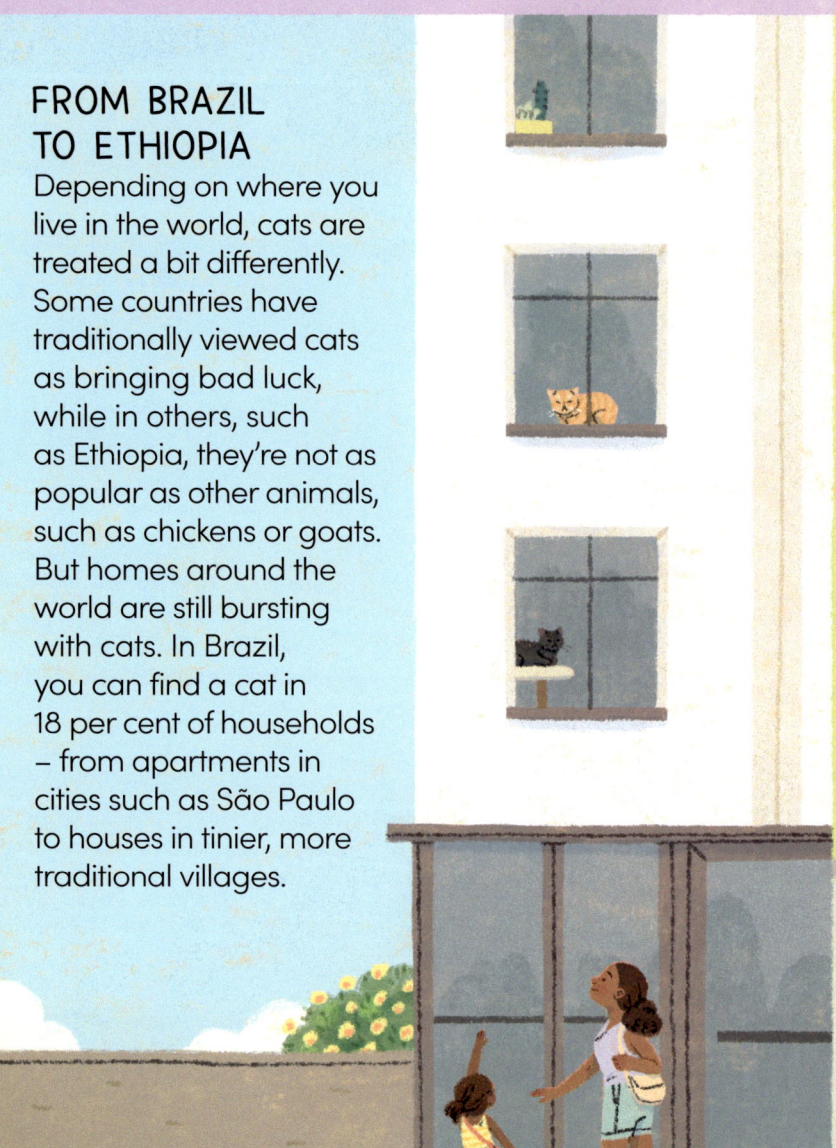

CITY CATS

In China, cat ownership has skyrocketed in recent years. Many people live in cities and it's easier to keep cats in smaller spaces than it is to keep dogs. Thanks to this, the cat food industry in China is booming!

CAT COMMUNITIES

While the life of a **stray cat** is difficult in most countries, in places such as Istanbul, Turkey, stray **cat colonies** are often treated like 'communal pets', with lots of love and care.

HOW DO YOU SAY 'CAT'?

In Swahili, you say 'paka'. In Arabic, there's a 'qita' lapping water from her bowl. In Korean, a 'goyang-i' is chasing that mouse toy.

INDOORS OR OUTDOORS?

In Australia and New Zealand, there's an important debate: *Should we keep our cats indoors to save the wildlife?* **Feral cats** are also contributing to the problem of endangered species (animals at risk of disappearing entirely).

Cats are sometimes fitted with **microchips** to identify them if they get lost. In France, one cat named Angie was lost for *11 years*. Luckily, she had a happy reunion with her owner, thanks to the microchip that told a vet: *Yep, this is Angie!*

OUTSIDE DANGERS

Pet guardians in Canada and the United States of America are also divided on the issue of letting their cats outdoors. Is that a safe thing to do? Some argue that it makes them happier and improves their wellbeing, while others say there are too many dangers – such as cars and wild animals – for house cats to face outside.

In Japan, some islands have more cats than people – and these places have become tourist attractions! People flock to take pictures with the island's strays. Aoshima Island in southern Japan boasts 100 cats for every 15 people! How did all these cats get there in the first place? While no one knows for sure, some people say that these kitties were brought on to fishing boats to help cut down on the number of mice, then ended up on the islands and never left.

CATS IN ANCIENT EGYPT

Picture the scene – more than 5,000 years ago an ancient Egyptian family are out on a walk, when a snake appears. Then, a cat slinks from behind a rock, pouncing on the cobra and killing it, saving the family from harm. This is one reason why the ancient Egyptians were so obsessed with cats. Sharp-clawed, fast and fearless, they kept mice from destroying grain – and they protected humans from snakes and scorpions.

GODS AND MUMMIES

Some people claim that the ancient Egyptians worshipped cats, but that's not really the case. Instead, they worshipped many gods, a few of whom took the form of cats – such as Bastet, the goddess of protection and the home. In paintings, Bastet often has the head of a black cat, and according to stories, she was sometimes gentle, sometimes ready to attack – just like kitties you might know!

BASTET

THE HIGH LIFE
Cats belonging to ancient Egyptian royals often lived lavish lifestyles, licking food off special plates and wearing gold jewellery!

Cats were so special that many rulers kept them as pets – such as Prince Thutmose and his cat Ta-Miu, who was buried next to him in a special **sarcophagus**. Lots of people in ancient Egypt were buried with cats, or with cats nearby.

Some of these kitties were mummified – prepared for the afterlife in a ritual process that included wrapping them in linens. Did you know that the oldest pet cemetery ever was in ancient Egypt? Over 500 kitties are buried there, along with some dogs and other animals, too.

GOODBYE, EYEBROWS
Many people in ancient Egypt were so attached to their cats that when the cat died, they shaved their own eyebrows as a sign of grief. Imagine walking up to someone in the street and thinking: *Oh, you have no eyebrows! Your cat must've died!*

Unless it was for mummification, killing a cat was a *huge* no-no. Not only was it against the law, it was also punishable by death – even if the cat died accidentally.

A LEGENDARY BATTLE
Depictions of cats and cat life are stamped all over Egypt. A tomb scene at Thebes, a city in ancient Egypt, shows a kitty catching a bird in her mouth and two others with her paws.

CAT SHIELDS
Cats live on in stories, too. There's a legend – passed down for centuries – that when the Persians (another group of ancient people, from Iran) met the Egyptians for battle in the city of Pelusium, the Persians painted cats on their shields. The Persians knew the Egyptians would never attack the image of their own cat gods. They were right – the Egyptians surrendered and lost the battle.

TALES OF ANCIENT HISTORY

Like the ancient Egyptians, many other cultures worshipped cat gods, or gods who appeared in cat-like forms. Especially . . . jaguars!

THE JAGUAR GODS

In the 1300s, the Aztec people lived in the area known today as Mexico. They looked to dozens of gods for strength, including Tezcatlipoca, god of the night sky. The night sky is almost like the silky coat of a jaguar, speckled with stars (like spots), and that's how Tezcatlipoca is often shown in early artwork – as a jaguar-headed god.

Going further back, the Mayans, who lived in today's Mexico, Guatemala and Belize from 2000 BCE to 1600 CE, had a host of jaguar gods, including one known as the Jaguar God of the Underworld.

TEZCATLIPOCA

I BLAME YOU!
"The cat did it" is an ancient Greek phrase! Born in 446 BCE, the playwright Aristophanes often wrote about cats with a curious streak who got blamed for light chaos.

SYMBOLS OF FREEDOM

You know how a cat is sometimes aloof – walking around on her own, not particularly caring what people think? The ancient Greeks and the ancient Romans loved that independence. Cats became symbols of freedom and were honoured in ways that other animals were not. Ferrets? Great for catching mice. But cats? Cats were allowed inside sacred Roman temples, unlike ferrets and weasels.

WORK OF ART

In the ancient Roman city of Pompeii, which was covered by lava and ash in 79 CE after a nearby volcano erupted, archeologists have discovered the most wonderful mosaic of a little spotted kitty, proudly showing off the quail (a type of bird) that she's pounced on.

ANCIENT CAT TALES

Almost 7,000 kilometres away from Rome, in India, cats also have a long history. Ancient tales such as *The Mahabharata* and *The Ramayana* – both written around 2,500 years ago – showcase kitties in exciting life-and-death moments. Have you ever heard of the tale *Puss in Boots*, about a tricksy cat and his charming shoes? It is thought to have originated from an Indian folktale, created around the same time as *The Mahabharata*.

A POET'S CAT

Travel back to ancient China in 1183 and you might see a poet named Lu You at his desk. He's shooing away rats, muttering: "Begone! Stop chewing my books!" He hangs his head in despair before having a wonderful idea: *I'll buy a cat.* Interestingly, the poet didn't buy his kitten with money – but with a bag of salt. That's a pretty good trade!

It certainly was for Lu You, who gained inspiration from cat ownership. After that, many of his poems revolved around all the cats he bought, who *did* save his books, and made Lu You wait on them hand and foot – or paw and paw!

ARE BLACK CATS UNLUCKY?

All across the world, people have different traditions during the festive season. Some light candles, others sing songs. In Iceland, they await the arrival of the Yule Cat.

BIG, HUNGRY CATS

According to legend, the Yule Cat – called 'Jólakötturinn' in the Icelandic language – isn't as friendly as Father Christmas! Instead, he peers into homes before Christmas dinner, seeing which children have received new clothes as presents. If they have received new clothes, that means they've been 'good' and have done as their parents have asked. No clothes? Well, that means you're a 'lazy' child who hasn't completed your chores, and the Yule Cat will eat your Christmas dinner – then eat you for dessert!

Did I mention that the Yule Cat is as big as a house?

SCARY CATS

Stories of enormous, thieving cats have been around for ages. Look no further than the Cat-Sìth from Scottish and Irish lore, black with a white spot on his chest, and as big as a dog. People thought that he'd show up at funerals! They were so afraid of him, family members would sometimes wrestle in front of the coffin, thinking: *The Cat-Sìth won't steal the soul of Uncle Hamish if we're distracting him like this!* Maybe the cat would even . . . like some **catnip**? Best to throw some around.

WITCHES IN DISGUISE?

Historically, why have so many people associated cats with terrible things? It seems really unfair, and it is! As humans, sometimes, we're just afraid of animals that we don't totally understand – and cats can be very mysterious creatures.

In the Middle Ages, a large span of time from around 1500 to 500 years ago, some people started to associate cats – black cats, in particular – with witches. Maybe all black cats were witches in disguise? Maybe they were sent to do a witch's evil bidding? It got so bad that cats were even blamed for the **bubonic plague**! What's especially unfair is that cats were actually helping to get *rid* of the plague – which was caused by fleas, carried on mice and rats.

> **THE BLACK DEATH**
> A plague is a disease caused by bacteria that can make lots of people and animals very sick. The first wave of the bubonic plague, also known as the Black Death, swept across Europe in 1347. Luckily, there's a cure for it now!

BLACK CATS NEED LOVE, TOO!

Even today, black cats are still associated with witchy holidays such as Halloween, and they are less likely to be adopted from shelters. Some people think that crossing paths with a black cat will bring them bad luck, but really, maybe that kitty was just trying to say hello! Go ahead, give her a little stroke under the chin. Maybe that'll bring you *good* luck!

DO CATS HAVE NINE LIVES?

Horseshoes, four-leaf clovers, ladybirds and . . . cats? What do they all have in common? Funnily enough, even though some people think that cats are unlucky, others consider them very lucky indeed!

EXTRA TOES, EXTRA LUCK
Sailors in the 1600s favoured **polydactyl cats** – ones with extra toes. Ship's captains brought them aboard – the more toes, the better, when it comes to catching mice and rats. Boats also sailed more smoothly on stormy seas if these cats were aboard, so the superstition goes.

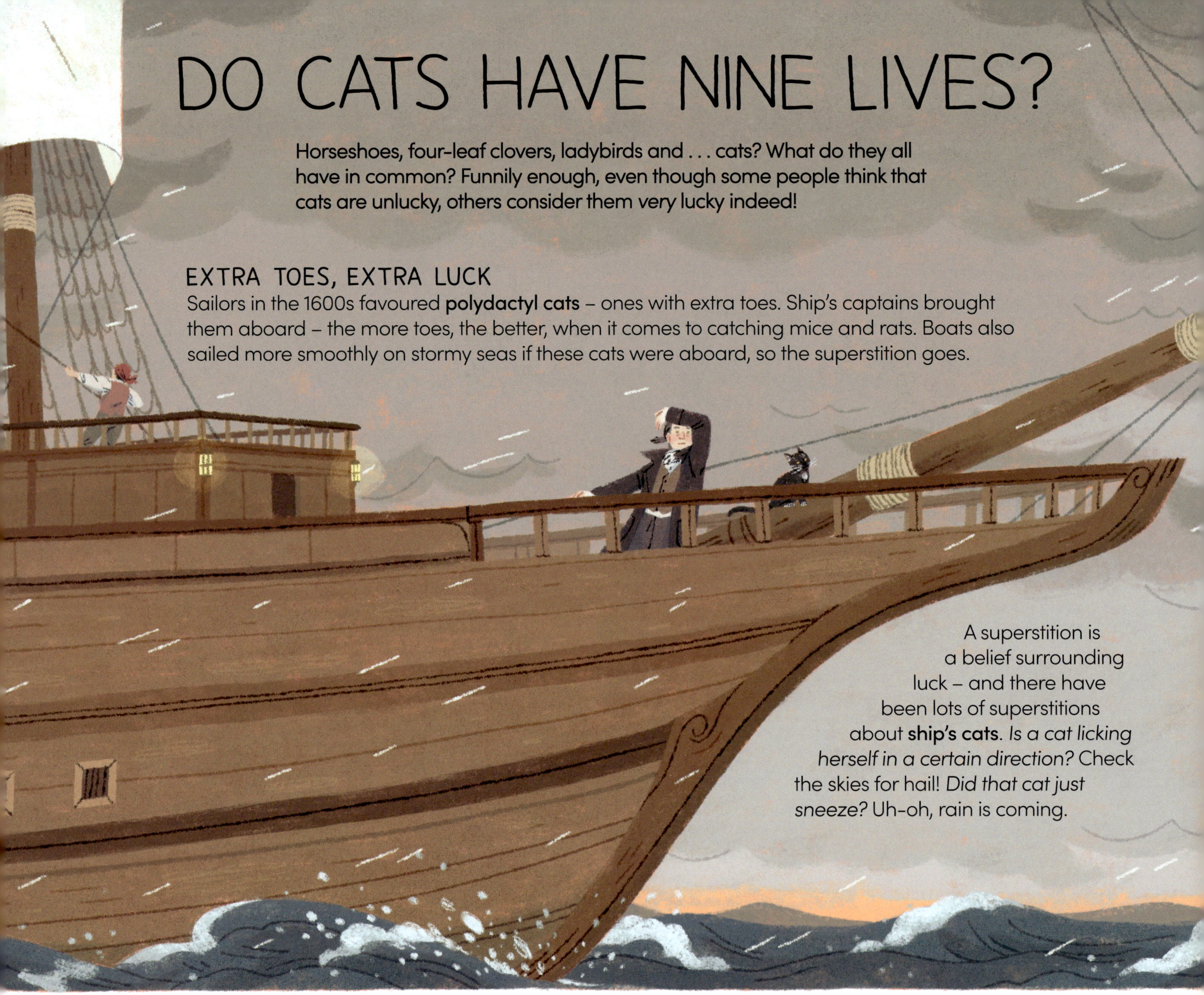

A superstition is a belief surrounding luck – and there have been lots of superstitions about **ship's cats**. *Is a cat licking herself in a certain direction? Check the skies for hail! Did that cat just sneeze? Uh-oh, rain is coming.*

How silly is that? Well, actually, not that silly. Cats really are sensitive to weather. If you have a cat, maybe you've noticed her ears prick up before a storm – before you hear the rumble of thunder. She's heard the storm brewing, smelled the rain in the air and felt the change in the air pressure, deep in her ears.

COME HERE FOR GOOD LUCK!

Have you ever seen a cute little white or gold cat statue waving a paw at you? That's the beckoning cat, called 'maneki-neko' in Japanese, and that wave isn't *really* a wave. The kitty is actually beckoning you forward, drawing you closer, saying: *Come here, come here, good luck is this way.*

So, what's the story here? In Japan, hundreds of years ago, a ruler was out hunting – paying attention only to his **prey** and to his falcons – when he saw a little kitty named Tama, perched inside the Gōtoku-ji temple. Then, the cat started beckoning him closer. Obeying the cat, the ruler stepped inside the temple – right before lightning struck the exact spot where he once stood. He thought: *This cat has saved my life!*

Today, people place these figurines in their homes for good luck.

NINE TIMES LUCKY

Cats are also seen to be lucky in their own lives. Have you ever heard the expression "a cat has nine lives"? Some people believe this saying was coined by English playwright William Shakespeare, who was born in Stratford-upon-Avon in 1564. "Good king of cats", is how one character refers to another in Shakespeare's famous play, *Romeo and Juliet*, before asking him for one of his "nine lives".

LITTLE CHARMERS
Although black cats are sometimes unfairly associated with bad luck, one Welsh saying says the opposite! In 1897, the popular rhyme proclaimed: "A black cat, I've heard it said / Can charm all ill away."

CATS RULE!

In ancient Egypt, cats held a special place in the homes of pharaohs (rulers of the land). And cats might have got a taste for this high status! Throughout history, many important people – from religious leaders to presidents – have had cats by their sides.

CATS OF THE POPE

All the way back in the 1820s, a little grey-and-red cat was making a name for himself, and that name was Micetto! His guardian, Pope Leo XII – the worldwide leader of the Catholic church at that time – let him climb on his lap during meetings, and legend has it that he often hid inside the Pope's garments.

Many years later, kitties named Chico and Contessina followed in Micetto's pawsteps. They lounged around the Vatican, where the Pope lives, receiving nice pats from Pope Benedict XVI, who was a real cat lover. On one occasion, a whole *group* of **stray cats** trailed the Pope to his residence. That's probably because he was known to feed them – and have long chats with them!

DINNER GUESTS AND LOTS OF PRESS

When Abraham Lincoln – the 16th president of the United States of America – ate dinner in the mid 1800s, guess who also dined at his table? It may be just a story, but lots of people claim that Lincoln fed his cats, Dixie and Tabby, on special dishes at the table. He believed they deserved the same treatment as the members of his government!

Dixie and Tabby might have been the first pet cats in the White House, where all US presidents live, but they certainly weren't the last. Socks, the black-and-white kitty of President Bill Clinton, liked to perch on top of podiums. He was so popular, the Clinton family had to tell the newspaper photographers to leave him alone.

A QUEEN'S KITTIES
In 1792, Marie Antoinette, queen of France, tried to escape the country when her life was in danger. She never made it onto the boat bound for Maine in the United States of America, but some stories say that her cats did! Those fluffy Angoras might be the ancestors of today's equally fluffy Maine Coons.

FROM STRAY TO NATIONAL TREASURE
Then, there's the most important job in the British government – the Chief Mouser of Number 10 Downing Street, where the Prime Minister lives. For hundreds of years, a series of kitties have tackled this demanding role, scaring away rodents from the Prime Minister's home and work place. Chief Mouser Larry is one of the longest serving cats. Staying in office longer than most leaders, he is known for taking his job very seriously – once, he even chased away a *fox*!

BRAVE CATS

All cats are a little bit fearless. They climb to great heights! Stand up to much bigger animals! Attack toys with gusto! But some kitties – especially those on ships – have gone down in history for their bravery.

THE CAT WHO WOULDN'T SINK

Legend has it that in 1941, during the Second World War, British sailors spied something . . . floating. One called out, "Is that a cat in the water, clinging to a plank of wood?" The cat had survived the sinking of an enemy ship, and British soldiers welcomed him into their ranks – giving him the name Oscar. 'Oscar,' you see, stands for 'man overboard' in military code.

That would've been a remarkable story in and of itself. But soon afterwards, Oscar – who either had very good or very terrible luck – found himself on a second sinking ship. Yet again, there he was, in the water! As you might know, cats aren't huge fans of water – he must have been very cross. So, he boarded another British ship . . . which *also* sank. And Oscar also survived! By this time, he'd become a legend, earning another name – Unsinkable Sam.

WELL-DRESSED SOLDIERS

Another brave kitty named Simon was the only cat to ever receive the Dickin Medal, the highest honour for animals in wartime Britain. Found as a **stray** – scouring the docks for food – Simon met a British sailor who took one look at the black-and-white furball and thought: *You'd be a good **ship's cat**! I'm sneaking you onboard.* From then on, Simon valiantly patrolled his vessel, ridding it of mice, and kept morale up after an attack on the ship.

Don't forget about Pooli! Born at Pearl Harbor, a U.S. naval base near Hawaii, she was another Second World War kitty who served valiantly, never once abandoning ship. She even had her own tiny military uniform, complete with ribbons and battle stars.

THE ONLY CAT ASTRONAUT

Many people have heard the story of Laika, the first dog in space. Some have even heard of Ham, a great ape who travelled the skies for NASA. But I bet you didn't know that before France sent human astronauts into space, they first sent a cat.

She is thought to have started her life as a street cat from Paris. One day, researchers scooped her up and brought her in for training, making her do many scary and uncomfortable tasks, such as spinning around very fast in a machine. In 1963, she was eventually tucked into a capsule (a teeny-tiny space ship) and launched into orbit. Miraculously, she survived – landing back on Earth thanks to a miniature parachute. French newspapers and TV reporters loved her.

CATS IN SCIENCE

Are some cats . . . scientists? Maybe not in the traditional sense, but cats have been involved in some of the world's greatest scientific advances.

THE SPARK OF AN IDEA

Born in the country we now call Croatia, Serbian-American engineer Nikola Tesla developed new ways to transmit electricity safely. This allows us to power everything from lightbulbs to refrigerators and without his work, life would be very different today.

However, as a child, he was just a boy who loved his cat. Black, sleek and adventurous, his cat Macak followed Tesla wherever he went. According to one letter from 1939, Tesla claimed that he and Macak "lived for one another".

And Macak is a big reason why Tesla became so interested in science. One day in his home town, there was a tremendously bad storm, with lightning in the air – and when Tesla stroked Macak's back, sparks jumped! From then on, he was fascinated with electricity.

MIDNIGHT SNACKS

Edwin Hubble – the inventor of the Hubble telescope, a powerful tool to see into deep space – rarely smiled in photos. The only time he did, he was with his half-Persian cat, Nicolas Copernicus, named after the famous astronomer from the 1300s. Nicolas Copernicus (the cat) gave Hubble plenty of reasons to grin – the cat lounged on his books and curled in his lap while Hubble conducted important scientific research. Like other astronomers, noted Hubble's wife, the kitty also stayed up late and enjoyed a nice snack in the moonlight!

CAT FLAPS

Let's turn to another famous scientist, Sir Isaac Newton. You may know him as the man who proposed the theory of gravity, but legend has it that he *also* invented the cat flap. That's not quite right, since the first mention of a cat door is in Geoffrey Chaucer's *The Canterbury Tales* – a series of stories published more than 150 years before Newton was even born. But it's still fun to think about Newton cutting holes in the door, allowing the cats to dart in and out so that they wouldn't keep interrupting his experiments!

OPERATION COPYCAT

You may have heard of **cloned** sheep, but have you heard of the world's first cloned pet? Short for Carbon Copy, her name was C.C., and she was – you guessed it! – a cat. Unexpectedly, C.C. didn't end up looking exactly like Rainbow, the cat from which she was cloned. But C.C. was still really cute and lived a long, healthy life!

C.C.    RAINBOW

CARBON COPY
Cloning is the process of taking cells from one animal and creating another identical or near-identical animal from those cells.

THE BIONIC CAT

A British cat named Oscar was the very first cat to receive two bionic feet. At just two years old, he lost his back feet in a farming accident in 2009 – but a veterinary surgeon was able to attach two titanium paws to his bones, allowing Oscar to run and even climb.

CATS AND CULTURE

Since the beginning of human history, works of art have reflected what we notice, fear, and appreciate. And what we appreciate is sometimes . . . a cat! Cave paintings found in France, believed to be up to 36,000 years old, show just how long we've been obsessed with cats. On one wall, five big lion heads – all with unique expressions – almost jump out from the rock.

SERIOUS CATS AND HAPPY CATS

Cats make natural subjects for artwork – they're interesting, beautiful and their fur captures the light. Sometimes they're painted with their human guardians, as in French artist Pierre-Auguste Renoir's *Child with Cat* (1887). The cat looks so warm and snuggly in the girl's arms, and it's clear that the two are friends.

In other works of art, such as Spanish artist Pablo Picasso's *Cat Catching a Bird* (1939), cats are used to represent real events happening in the world at the time. Picasso's cat is painted in the dullest brown. The darkness of the cat represents the war that raged in Spain during Picasso's lifetime.

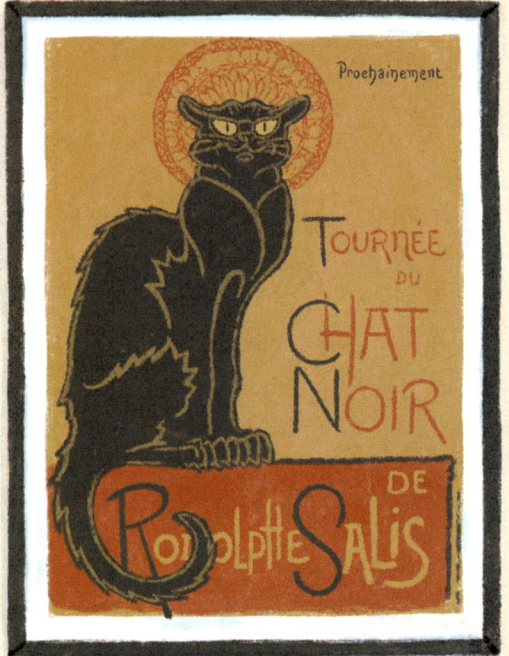

But art is not always that serious. Look at Chinese artist Men Zhen's *Black Cat*. Created all the way back in the 1700s, you'll see a smiling cat who has happily eaten many a good meal.

French painter Théophile Steinlen's *Tournée du Chat Noir* (1896) was created to advertise a popular cabaret (a club with a stage for performances) in Paris, France.

CAROL SINGING CATS?

English artist Louis Wain's cats, too, are full of fun and life – brightly coloured and big-eyed. Wain was obsessed with kitties and often painted them in human scenarios, such as carol singing at Christmas, playing card games and giving important lectures.

A BRIGHT IDEA

You may know Thomas Edison as the inventor of the light bulb. But that wasn't his only bright idea! He was also a fan of making short films. In fact, in 1894 he made a video featuring two circus cats 'boxing' in miniature gloves, inside a miniature ring, as a referee guides them. People adored the film! And it may have started the world's obsession with funny cat videos. Today, they are some of the most-watched – and most-loved – clips on the internet.

INTERNET MASCOTS
Some kitties have become internet celebrities, such as brown-and-white Tardar Sauce (better known by her nickname 'Grumpy Cat') and a Scottish Fold called Maru.

THE LASAGNE-EATER

Cats can also be found on the printed page, in magazines, books (such as the one you are reading now!) and even newspapers. Flip to the comic section to discover a famous lasagne-eating cat, who first appeared in US newspapers in 1978. His name is Garfield. He's big, beautiful and orange. And his American creator, Jim Davis, is no stranger to cat behaviour. When he was a little boy, Davis lived on a farm with 25 cats and liked to watch the ample-bodied house cats who lounged on armchairs inside. These real-life kitties inspired a legend.

BIG-HEARTED CATS

Meet Room 8, a cat with a story as lovely as his personality. The children at Elysian Heights Elementary School, in California in the United States of America, found him inside their classroom – which is where his name comes from. He'd managed to pitter-patter in through an open window.

Although he was a **stray**, this charming cat with a white bib made himself right at home – wandering the halls, greeting students and offering his head for gentle strokes.

Room 8 would even sit with the children at lunchtime, as they offered him bits of their packed lunches. Day after day he returned, all throughout the school year in 1952.

When the summer holidays came, he left – just like the students – and came back in the autumn for the start of a new term. This continued for so many years that Room 8 became a symbol of the school. Children from all across the country wrote him letters, inspired by his love for learning – and the way he made school seem a little less scary.

A KITTY BUSKER

Bob is one of the most famous street cats of all time – and this is all down to his heart. Marmalade-coloured Bob's life wasn't looking so good until guardian James Bowen found him in his building. The poor kitty had been injured and abandoned, and Bowen – a street busker in London, England – scooped him up and nursed him back to health.

Bob repaid the kindness with love – and showmanship. Often wearing his signature red scarf, he'd perch on Bowen's shoulder or in his guitar case during performances, drawing in crowds. Bowen might have saved Bob – but thanks to his constant companionship and sunny personality, Bob saved his human, too.

LOOKALIKES
In the movie version of this story, A Street Cat Named Bob, Bob played himself! There were also five other marmalade cats, acting as his stand-ins.

SCARLETT SAVES HER KITTENS

Some kitties show their hearts with acts of courage. In 1996, Scarlett captured the world's attention when she rescued her five kittens – one by one – during a garage fire in Brooklyn, New York. This mamma cat kept darting through flames, picking her kittens up by the scruff, and bringing them to safety.

One of the firemen on the scene, who happened to love animals, brought her to a rescue centre – where letters and phone calls started to pour in. People wanted to know: How was Scarlett doing? Was she going to be okay? Although Scarlett's fur was singed and her eyes damaged, she survived – and the kitty family was safely rehomed.

THE RICH AND THE FAMOUS

While some cats make headlines for their courage, appearance or historical significance, others stick in our minds for more unusual reasons. Let's meet some of them!

KITTY MILLIONAIRE

Tommaso might have looked like your average black cat – sleek fur, expressive yellow eyes – but there was something *slightly* different about him. He became one of the richest cats in the world.

In his early life, Tommaso was a **stray** – as many good cats are – wandering the streets of Rome in Italy. Tommaso's guardian fell in love with him, bringing him home. Sadly, years later, she passed away at the age of 94 and, to many people's surprise, left her £8 million fortune to Tommaso!

Now, you can't *really* leave money to your cat. So, Tommaso got to live a life of kitty luxury, with his money handled for him by someone his owner trusted deeply. Another animal lover, she was asked to provide for Tommaso until his dying day.

SOMETHING TO SING ABOUT

According to a list of the richest pets in the world, Olivia Benson – one of American singer-songwriter Taylor Swift's cats – has an estimated wealth of £73 million.

A GUEST AT THE END

In a nursing home in New Jersey in the United States of America, a doctor makes a phone call: "I'm sorry," he says. "You need to get here right away. Oscar, the cat, has just sat on the edge of your grandfather's bed." For most cats, bed-sitting isn't really anything to pay attention to – but with Oscar, it was a sign. Usually, he kept to himself and was not a cuddly cat. He only curled up with nursing home patients in the moments before they died.

This happened about *fifty* times. Fifty times, Oscar predicted: *This person doesn't have long to live.* He was so accurate that the doctors called in family members to say their goodbyes – and many thanked Oscar. He allowed them a few last moments with their loved ones.

So, how did Oscar do it? Some say he probably smelled a change in the dying people's cells – the tiniest building blocks in our bodies. Now, scientists are trying to figure out how AI (artificially intelligent machines) might learn to do the same thing.

A STAR IS BORN

Speaking of Oscars, do you know what the Oscars are? They are an awards ceremony, held in Hollywood in the United States of America, for the best actors and contributors to movies. And guess what? There's a version for animals!

Called the Patsy Award, it's given to outstanding animal performers – and Orangey, a marmalade cat, won it twice. Most famously, he starred in *Breakfast at Tiffany's* in 1961 alongside movie icon Audrey Hepburn.

73

DO CATS HAVE JOBS?

Cats might not seem like the hardest workers, especially if a human is trying to tell them what to do! But some cats take on important – and fun – roles.

THE FLUFFIEST STATION MASTER IN JAPAN

In the late 1990s, one railway line in Japan didn't have many passengers – but it did have a **tortoiseshell** kitty named Tama, who'd often show up at one of the stations. "Good cat", commuters would tell her as they passed, stroking her head. She became so popular that one of the rail workers had an idea: *What if this cat became the station master, the face of the railway?*

It turned out to be an exceptional idea! Tama really took to the position, saying hello to passengers with lots of affection. She even wore a tiny conductor's hat! And guess what? Business on the railway improved. One little kitty brought in tens of thousands of extra people.

THE MAIL CATS

From the 1860s, the Royal Mail in the United Kingdom hired cats to stop mice from chewing up the letters and parcels. 'Paid' at least a shilling a week, which went towards looking after them, these cats kept the mail rooms in order – but none more than Tibs, known as Tibs the Great, who weighed in at over 10 kilograms at his heaviest. Tibs took his job very seriously, staying in the role for 14 years!

> **NOT SO SPECIAL DELIVERY!**
> In Belgium, in the 1870s, a *brilliant* plan was thought up: *Let's put people's post in tiny bags, hang them around cats' necks, and those cats can deliver the bags to their homes!* Okay, okay – maybe this idea wasn't so brilliant. All 37 cats did make it home, but at a too-slow pace – way, way too slow. The experiment was an adorable failure.

LOCAL CELEBRITY

In Alaska in the United States of America, there's a small town called Talkeetna. In 1997, residents there decided that no one could run their town better than Stubbs. Stubbs, however, was not a human. Stubbs was a kitten.

After being voted in, Stubbs became the mayor! For many years, this pale ginger cat served with dignity and a sparkling personality, meeting people at the local shop. Humans could give him a quick stroke on the back, and he'd give them a reassuring head-butt in return. What more could you ask for in a leader?

STARRING ROLE

In London, England, people at the Gielgud Theatre remember Beerbohm, a celebrity in the theatre world from the 1970s to the early 1990s. Beerbohm was supposed to stay behind the scenes, catching mice, but he'd often scurry onstage during performances and visit actors in their dressing rooms, as if to say: *Good evening, and break a leg out there!*

FEELING BETTER WITH CATS

Whenever you stroke a nice cat and that cat purrs and looks up at you with happiness, you're probably going to feel happy, too!

WHAT DOES IT TAKE TO BECOME A THERAPY CAT?

You might have heard of therapy dogs, who go into public places such as schools, hospitals and nursing homes to bring people comfort and support – but did you know that cats are also great for therapy?

These kitties have to be really confident! New places mean lots of new people, smells, sounds and sights – and they can't be scared of them. In most cases, they also have to walk well in a harness and a lead – which almost any cat can do, if trained properly.

And, of course, a friendly and outgoing personality is a must for **therapy cats**!

HOSPITALS AND AIRPORTS

Duke Ellington Morris, from California in the United States of America, started life as a **feral** kitten, before he was adopted by an owner who noticed he was very laid back and might make a good therapy cat.

Soon he was working in the intensive care unit (ICU) of a hospital, being pushed around the wards on a little cart and extending his muzzle for a nice under-the-chin scratch from each patient. From there, he started working at an airport, comforting nervous travellers: *You don't have to be afraid of flying. Here, stroke me instead!*

OFFICE CATS

In offices, too, cats can provide comfort, joy and stress relief. Peek into the windows of one company in Japan, and you'll find cats trotting along the computer desks! These rescue kitties brighten up the office with their wonderful personalities, and make the employees a lot happier. Employees can bring their own cats to work as well.

YOU HAVE A CALL!

Ring, ring! That's the telephone. Zebby, a clever black-and-white cat from Derbyshire in England, hears the sound – and gently taps his paw against his human's face. Zebby's owner is deaf and uses hearing aids. With Zebby's help, she knows when to put them in when it's time to take a call. If there's someone at the door – or even a strange noise in the night – Zebby will alert her then, too.

The remarkable thing is, Zebby hasn't had any training, but he still gives these alerts – *and* does things such as fetch slippers and the post!

FACT OR FICTION?

Here are some statements that people believe about cats. But what's fact, and what's fiction?

CATS ALWAYS LAND ON THEIR FEET
Cats have an incredible ability to 'right' themselves, twisting and turning through the air and landing paws-first on the ground. Even three-week-old kittens have a hint of this 'righting reflex'! But cats don't *always* manage the perfect landing – if they fall from a very short height, there isn't enough time to spin around.

CATS CAN SEE IN COMPLETE DARKNESS
Nope! Not complete darkness. They need at least a *little* bit of light to pass through their eyes, but they can still navigate pretty well – in a totally dark room – with just their whiskers.

CATS HATE SWIMMING – AND WATER!
If a cat accidentally falls into a lake, what will happen? Can she swim? The answer . . . yes! Funnily enough, in emergencies kitties do the *doggy* paddle. Instinct tells them to move their paws in order to push forward through the water. However, in general, cats really don't *like* to swim. A soggy cat isn't a happy cat.

CATS SHOULD DRINK MILK

Kittens thrive on their mother's milk. In fact, they only transition to solid food at around four weeks old. Maybe that's why we often think shop-bought milk (usually cow's milk) is good for them. However, cats are actually lactose intolerant! That means drinking milk will give them a bad tummy.

PREGNANT PEOPLE SHOULDN'T BE AROUND CATS

When people are pregnant, they're at increased risk of getting a harmful infection called **toxoplasmosis** – which you can pick up from cat poo. Toxoplasmosis is not good for babies growing inside the womb. So, when people get pregnant, all they have to do is ask someone else to clean the litter box – but they can still cuddle with their cats, and give them plenty of love!

CATS ARE LESS FRIENDLY THAN DOGS

Certainly not! It's more that, as humans, we can see the friendliness of dogs easily. Dogs give big wags of their tails and long, slobbery face licks. Dogs also need us more, for just about everything! And therefore, they're constantly at our sides. Cats express their friendliness in different, sometimes less noticeable ways – slow blinking, for example, or a very quiet purr.

Unlike dogs, cats can do quite well on their own. So, many don't feel the need to be around us 24/7. That doesn't mean they're unfriendly! Cats, like our other furry friends, can be incredibly warm, kind and sociable.

CATS EVERYWHERE

Everywhere you look, cats are out and about. In cat shows, kitties compete to take home ribbons, proving they're the 'best' example of their **breed**, while places such as cat cafés let you meet kitties over lunch.

10 OUT OF 10

From Thailand to Spain, cat shows take place all around the world. Siamese cats! Persians! Maine Coons! They lie, strut and purr before the judges, who pick them up, examining them from whiskers to tail. "This cat", a judge might say, "has exactly the right coat texture and markings for a Maine Coon – I award him a score of 10!" Mostly, it is **purebred** cats who take part in these shows – but on occasion, **mixed-breed** cats are also welcome. These cats are judged, at least in part, on how friendly they are.

There are prizes for the overall winner, each breed, and even 'best kitten' – a young cat who is already showing how 'perfectly' they represent the breed.

Some people are *really* competitive – and work very hard for their cats to bring home that ribbon. They'll feed their cats special food, and groom them daily!

COFFEE WITH CATS

Have you ever heard of a cat café? No, the kitties aren't wearing little aprons, and they're not serving you hot drinks – they're sitting on your lap or weaving around your feet while you eat.

You'll find cat cafés in oodles of countries, including Thailand, Germany and New Zealand. Japan has over 150 of them! Come inside, meet the kitties and play with them. Even if you don't have a cat at home, you can bond with one for an hour or two. Some cafés care more about making money than helping the kitties, but the better cafés do care about the cats – and even offer adoptions.

If you bond with a cat and are in a position to look after him, why not adopt him? You two can have tea together forever!

CAT CONVENTIONS

At cat shows, cats are the ones being shown off – but in many countries, cat conventions and festivals showcase a variety of things *for* cats. People set up booths with bright signs, advertising everything from the newest cat food to the shiniest new toys: *Look over here! Buy this cat tree that looks like a unicorn! And this electronic feather toy that'll keep your kitty entertained for hours!*

A ROBOT . . . FOR CATS?

New technology is coming out all the time – from high-tech toys to robotic litter trays! One litter tray even weighs your cat when she jumps in. When she's finished her business, the robotic device then sifts through the litter, giving her a clean space for next time.

THE LAP OF LUXURY

People love to spoil their cats, and – for the most part – cats love to be spoiled!

KINGS (AND QUEENS) OF THE JUNGLE

A **catio** is exactly like it sounds – a patio for cats that allows them to soak up the sun. Structures such as catios, cat trees and cat condos – little houses that cats can curl up in – are becoming more and more popular.

With built-in **scratching posts** and a number of high podiums, kitties can feel safe and keep their nails looking tidy. Some people take cat trees to the extreme – building walkable, wooden platforms throughout their house. It's like a miniature jungle, where cats can strut their stuff in the 'tree tops'. Cats love experiencing the world from up high, peering down and keeping an eye on things.

Take this house in Santa Barbara in the United States of America. It's designed by the founder of the House of Nekko, a rescue home for cats. Tip your chin up and gasp at the ceiling. Catwalks – high shelves for cats to walk on – are everywhere! There's even a miniature canoe hanging from the ceiling for cats to 'captain' from up high.

CAN CATS EAT... CAVIAR?

Some celebrities and rich people don't just pick their cat food off the supermarket shelves, they have it specially ordered for their pampered pets. One of the most expensive cat foods in the world is made with bits of real lobster, caviar (fancy fish eggs), salmon and crab. All the seafood is caught locally, so it's incredibly fresh. Even humans can try it! But you probably wouldn't want to . . .

Once your lucky kitty is finished with her lobster dinner, she can go for a spin on a fancy exercise wheel or play with some robotic mice. They'll zip and zoom, almost like the real thing.

SIMPLE THINGS, BEST THINGS

But there's no need to spend a lot of money to give your cats a life of luxury. All they want, really, is to curl up lovingly with you. Set up a comfy cat bed in a spot where sunlight streams through the window, toasting their furry little tummies, and they'll adore it.

For cats that stay indoors, many people also purchase birdfeeders, or build them from scraps of wood, and set them outside their windows. That way, cats will have something to watch. Birdfeeders are like kitty TV!

CAT QUIRKS

It's hard to deny the quirkiness of cats. Some of the things they do seem so odd – and so funny – to us. What's behind these little habits?

WHY DO CATS KNOCK OVER GLASSES?
That glass of water? That hair tie? It's going down. Some cats get bored, and what's more fun than making something move? Cats don't hunt non-moving things, so by putting an object in motion, they're kicking their instincts into overdrive. This is entertaining for them – and a little annoying for the human who has to clean up the mess!

WHY DOES MY CAT LICK MY HAIR?
Say you're on the sofa and you feel a strange sensation on the back of your head. It's a cat's tongue, working away at your scalp! Congratulations, your cat has decided to bond with you even more – by grooming you.

WHY DO CATS 'MAKE BISCUITS'?
Maybe it's happened to you – a cat kneading your jumper with her paws. It's like a lovely massage. We've talked about how cats are kind of like babies, and 'making biscuits' – as if they're little chefs, kneading dough – is what they do to get milk from their mothers. Also, it just feels nice on their paws! And it calms them down, putting them in a peaceful, trance-like state.

WHY DO CATS DRINK FROM THE TAP?

These types of videos are very popular on the internet – a cat walking up to a dripping tap and sticking her mouth right under it. Many cat quirks go back to their wild upbringing – the fact that they're only partly **domesticated**. In nature, flowing water is much more likely to be clean than a puddle that's been sitting there for ages, gathering bacteria. So, the flowing tap water is like a miniature stream or river. If your cats really like drinking from the tap, think about getting them a water bowl with a fountain.

WHY DOES MY CAT CURL UP IN MY DIRTY LAUNDRY?

Congratulations again! She loves you so much, she's attracted to your smell – which, to her, is quite strong!

WHY DO CATS DRINK SEAWATER?

If we humans drink seawater, we'll get quite sick. But cats *can* drink salt water. Their **kidneys** will filter most of that salt right out. That's because the ancestors of today's cats couldn't always find fresh water – so they had to drink a bit of salt water to survive. They adapted! That doesn't mean it's great for them, though. Make sure to provide fresh, clean drinking water for your cats.

CAREERS WITH CATS

What do you want to be when you grow up? An astronaut, a ballet dancer, or maybe a chef? But have you ever considered working with cats?

CAT DETECTIVE

Let's say there's a sweet cat who – just recently – started scratching everyone in her household. This is where, after making sure that there are no medical problems, the vet might ask a **cat behaviourist** to step in.

Cat behaviourists will examine the cat's daily routines. What's new or uncomfortable in their environment? Just like us, cats can experience stress – and behaviourists can explain: "Your cat isn't really aggressive! She's just reacting to another cat who moved into the house and garden next door. Feed her away from the back door, in a quiet, safe place." After that, the cat's 'bad' behaviour will probably go away.

ANIMAL ADVOCATE

You could also be an **animal advocate** – spreading the word about ways to love, respect and care for all kinds of animals, including cats. One famous animal advocate from the United States of America is Hannah Shaw, also known as the Kitten Lady. She helps the most vulnerable kittens receive medical treatment and get adopted – and she educates many people about cat care.

CAMERA-READY

Do you understand what makes the *purr-fect* haircut? Maybe you could be a cat groomer! Sometimes a cat's fur gets tangled or matted, and they need a 'lion cut' – shaving everything but their head, their paws and the tip of their tail, so they look like a miniature lion. Once kittie is picture-perfect, it's time for a photoshoot. Are you really skilled with a camera? You could be a cat photographer!

A CUDDLY CAREER

If you like helping cats find their forever homes you could even work in an animal shelter or sanctuary. Sometimes, these workers are paid, and other times, they're volunteers. One man in Wisconsin in the United States of America is a professional 'cat napper' – he goes into his local sanctuary and takes naps with the cats!

GOLDEN OLDIES
As cats get older, they can develop more and more health problems that vets help with. Elderly kitties often have difficulties with their teeth, their eyes and their **kidneys**.

THE DOCTOR IS IN

When you think about careers with cats, the first thing that might pop into your mind is a vet. Like us, cats get sick and need medical treatment – and vets provide them with skilled care. There's a lot to learn if you want to be a vet, from cat **anatomy** to cat medicine. Some vets specialize only in cats, while others treat a wide variety of animals, from horses to guinea pigs.

WHAT TO DO IF YOU FIND A STRAY

If you ever come across a lost-looking cat, outside your house or in your garden, you might wonder: *How can I help them?*

HELP NEEDED?

If the cat seems lost, the first thing to figure out is if it is a **stray** or if it got lost and actually belongs to a family. An adult in your life might be able to help you make a 'paper collar' – where you write a message, including a grown-up's phone number, asking the cat's owner to contact you, before placing it around the cat's neck. That way you'll know if the cat already has a home.

HOW DO YOU SAY HI TO A NEW CAT?

Extend a finger first – gently and slowly. Does the kitty sniff your finger, or does she back away? Look at her body language. Many cats are scared if you approach them fast and from above – but, if she seems interested in your finger, maybe try to give her a slow scratch under her chin. Remember, never pick up or handle an unknown cat on your own.

If you don't hear anything for a few days, you could put up 'found' posters around your neighbourhood to raise awareness. If this still doesn't attract any information about the cat's owner, you could report the cat to your local animal shelter, or an adult might be able to put the cat in a carrier and take them to the vet – to check if they're **microchipped** and to see if they need any medical help.

FERAL CATS

You are less likely to spot a **feral cat** near your house, because they are scared of humans and tend to distance themselves from populated areas. If you do see one, they are unlikely to come close to you, even with encouragement. Normally it is best to let them be, but if they seem to be in need of medical care, you can ask an adult to contact a vet or shelter for advice.

LOOK! KITTENS!

In animal rescue, we call spring '**kitten season**'. Spring – and all throughout the summer – is when cats usually have their babies. If you find a **stray** mamma cat with her kittens, tell a trusted adult. Together, you can contact a local shelter and see if they have space for a few new cats.

Now that you've contacted the cat shelter, maybe you could even volunteer with them!

FOSTER FAMILY

Sometimes, when shelters are full, they'll ask for volunteers to foster cats. Fosterers bring kitties into their homes and give them lots of good food and cuddles, making those kitties comfortable before they find their forever homes.

A FOREVER HOME

So, if you'd like to make a cat a member of your family, what does that process look like? It can actually take many forms. Sometimes, cats just show up!

RESCUE CENTRES

In many cities and towns, there are rescue centres for cats who are looking for families of their own. You can meet lots of kitties, picking out the one – or two! – that you like best. In some places, you'll have to make an appointment, while in others, you can just walk in. Someone working there might ask your family questions such as "What are you looking for in a cat?".

They might suggest one or two options – "Here's Muzzy! Here's Lemon Meringue!" – or invite you to meet all the cats on your own. They might also ask you some questions about the people and pets already living in your home to check that it would be a good fit for the cat you've chosen. It's easy to fall in love with a shelter cat – and they'll be so grateful that you chose them. People often go for kittens – they're so tiny and adorable! – but older cats are just as cute and deserve the chance for love.

BREEDER

You can also purchase a cat from a breeder – someone who sells a certain type of cat, such as Siamese cats or Angoras. However, there are so many amazing cats who need homes, all over the world, so it's a great idea to check with shelters first.

A SAFE ROOM

When you bring a new kitty into your home, it can be overwhelming for them. So, it's a good idea to keep them in a 'safe room' to start with – a smaller room, such as a bathroom – where they can feel comfy, cosy and know exactly where their litter box, food dish and water bowl is. Once they've gained confidence, they can start to explore the rest of the house.

SWEETER BY THE PAIR
If you're thinking about adopting kittens, consider getting two! Kittens have lots of energy and need cat company. This way, they'll have a playmate.

In the first 48 hours especially, make sure your cat is drinking enough water. Cats can get dehydrated very quickly.

EVERY CAT IS A GOOD CAT

Maybe there's a cat purring on your lap right now. Maybe you're looking down at her with love – and you're thinking about everything you've just read, about the importance of her whiskers, the telling hum of her purr and the way her ancestors roamed the **Fertile Crescent**, thousands and thousands of years ago. "Did you know", you might whisper to her, "that the ancient Egyptians adored cats like you?"

TOGETHER FOREVER

Sure, cats might have minds of their own – and that's a good thing! – but they've also learned the quickest ways to our hearts: *If I meow like this, he'll feed me. If I rub my head against her ankles, she's mine forever.*

Because we *will* be together forever. It's impossible to imagine a world without cats. Their histories and our histories are intertwined – like two cats curled up together – and they'll continue to stay by our sides, standoffishly or not.

SCARLETT

SIMON

FLUFFY TEACHERS

I think we can learn a great deal from cats. We can learn courage from our kitty heroes – from Scarlett, who saved her kittens, and Simon the wartime **ship's cat**. We can learn kindness from kitties such as Room 8 and Bob the street cat, who opened their hearts to many, many people. And from all the cats in the world, throughout history and in legends, we can learn that we shouldn't judge – or fear – things we don't fully understand.

BOB

Cats might be tiny **predators**, but the biggest thing they've captured is our imaginations. It's amazing to think about all the things cats can do – from working in a post office, to cheering up hospital patients, to surviving a shipwreck multiple times. And we really are just scratching the surface when it comes to cats – who knows what scientists will find out about their brilliance in the future!

COOL TO BE A CAT

No cat is 'just' a cat. That's what my family's cat, Bella, has taught me. When she's snoozing on the sofa at night, her **polydactyl** paws twitching, I can tell she's having colourful dreams. I can tell, every time she gazes out a window, that there's a whole world between her ears.

Year after year, I'm learning more about her – and she never ceases to surprise me. I'll say her name, "Bella! Here, kitty-kitty!", and she'll rush from a far corner of the house, eager to have a chat. She'll head-butt me with love, and I'll slow blink at her in return. We're communicating. We're tightening our bond.

She might think I'm a big cat, but I'm okay with that. Being a cat – it turns out – is pretty cool.

GLOSSARY

ANATOMY The structure of the body.

ANIMAL ADVOCATE A person who spreads the word about ways to love, respect and care for animals.

BONDED PAIR Two cats who are so emotionally close, they would struggle if separated.

BREED A specific type of cat that looks, and usually acts, a certain way.

BUBONIC PLAGUE A disease – caused by bacteria – that made a lot of people and animals very sick. The first wave, also known as the Black Death, swept across Europe in 1347.

CANINE A pointy tooth that can tear meat apart.

CAT BEHAVIOURIST A person who examines a cat's daily routines to determine why they might be stressed.

CAT COLONY A group of up to 15 cats living together outside.

CATIO A patio for cats.

CATNIP A plant containing a chemical that stimulates a cat's brain and makes them happy.

CAT'S EYE REFLECTOR A road marker that reflects the headlights of vehicles, guiding traffic in low light.

CLONING The process of taking cells from one animal and creating another identical, or near-identical, animal from those cells.

COLLARBONES The curvy bones that connect shoulders to the rest of the body.

CREPUSCULAR Describing animals that are most active at twilight.

DOMESTICATE The process of turning a wild animal into a tame one.

EVOLVE To develop over a long span of time.

FELIDAE The cat family.

FELINE A cat, a member of the cat family or relating to cats.

FERAL CAT A cat who hasn't had much, or any, contact with people.

FERTILE CRESCENT An area of the Middle East where the land was particularly good for growing crops, and where cats were first domesticated.

FLEHMEN RESPONSE A behaviour where animals open their mouths, allowing them to *taste* smells.

FOLLICLE A very sensitive organ in a cat's skin, from which a hair or a whisker grows.

HAIRBALL A clump of hair that forms in the stomach of a cat when they have swallowed too much fur.

KERATIN A protein that makes up cat fur and whiskers, as well as human fingernails.

KIDNEYS Organs that flush toxins out of the body.

KITTEN SEASON Spring – and all throughout the summer – when cats usually have their babies.

MICROCHIP An electronic device used to identify an animal if they get lost.

MIXED-BREED A cat whose parents are different breeds.

MOGGY A mixed-breed cat.

MOLARS Teeth, alongside premolars, used to chew food.

NERVE A long, thin fibre that sends electrical signals to the brain or to other parts of the body.

OBLIGATE CARNIVORE An animal that needs meat to survive.

OLFACTORY RECEPTOR A special part of a cat's body, found in the nose, that translates odour particles into scents.

OXYTOCIN A hormone (or chemical message) released from your brain which makes you feel love.

PERIPHERAL VISION The ability to see things out of the corners of the eyes.

PHEROMONE A chemical marker produced by an animal to send messages to others of the same species.

PITCH How high or low a sound is.

POLYDACTYL CAT A cat with extra toes.

PREDATOR An animal that kills and eats other animals.

PREMOLARS Teeth, alongside molars, used to chew food.

PREY An animal hunted by other animals for food.

PUREBRED A cat whose ancestors were all the same breed.

SARCOPHAGUS A limestone coffin used in ancient Egypt.

SCRATCHING POST A stretch of wood or similar, often wrapped in rough material, that a cat can use to file down their nails.

SECURE ATTACHMENT A bond with a caregiver where an animal (or a person) feels safe.

SHIP'S CAT A cat that lives on a ship, usually brought on board to control the mouse and rat populations.

SOLICITING PURR A sound made by a cat, combining a cry with a nice, humming purr.

STRAY CAT A cat who once had contact with humans but is now out on their own.

TABBY CAT A cat with tiny 'M' markings on their forehead and a coat with a swirl of colours and shapes.

TERRITORY An area that a cat believes belongs to them.

THERAPY CAT A cat who goes into public places, such as schools, hospitals and nursing homes, to bring people comfort and support.

TORTOISESHELL CAT A cat whose coat includes a mix of two colours – such as orange and brown – with white.

TOXOPLASMOSIS A harmful infection that you can pick up from cat poo.

UPPER INCISORS The teeth on the top row between the sharpest, longest teeth.

VACCINE A type of medicine that stops people and animals from getting sick.

VERTEBRAE Back bones that make up a spine.

VOICE BOX The part of the throat where a human or animal's voice comes from. Also known as the larynx.

VOMERONASAL ORGAN A special organ that allows cats to taste smells.

INDEX

A
Adoption 36, 45, 59, 76, 80, 86, 91
American Curl 48
Angora 63, 90

B
Black cat 25, 54, 58-59, 61, 66, 68, 72
Black-and-white cat 58, 62, 65, 68, 77

C
Cat-Sìth 58
Chartreux 50
Chinese Lop-Eared 49
Cornish Rex 46, 51

E
Egyptian Mau 48

F
Feral 28, 42-43, 53, 76, 89

K
Kitten 3, 14, 17, 23, 24, 29, 31, 42-43, 46, 49, 51, 57, 71, 75, 76, 78-79, 80, 86, 89, 90-91, 92

L
LaPerm 51

M
Maine Coon 46-47, 63, 80
Manx 26
Moggy 44, 50
Munchkin 14, 46

N
Norwegian Forest 46, 49

O
Oriental Shorthair 51

P
Persian 45, 66, 80
Peterbald 51

R
Ragdoll 44
Russian Blue 44

S
Savannah 45
Scottish Fold 44, 69
Siamese 49, 50, 80, 90
Singapura 46
Sphynx 14, 44
Stray 42-43, 52-53, 62, 63, 65, 70, 72, 88-89

T
Tabby 20, 34, 45, 50
Tortoiseshell 17, 41, 45, 46, 74
Turkish Van 46

W
White cat 23, 61

Y
Yule Cat 58

Siberian Forest

Cornish Rex

Abyssinian

Bombay

Siamese

American Curl

Devon Rex

Birman

Havana Brown

Chinchilla

Peterbald

Manx

Savannah

Ocicat

Korat